DrRina
COUNSELLING PSYCH(

CW00545688

THE
MAGIC
IN ME

Transform your relationship
with yourself and the key people
in your life

R^ethink

First published in Great Britain in 2023
by Rethink Press
www.rethinkpress.com

Cover image © Adobe Stock | sarayut_sy

Contents

I would like to thank those who have been a part of shaping my journey – from my family to my friends, my colleagues and my respected clients. I am also grateful for the people who have challenged me. Thank you for helping me to stop and reflect. Every day you make me want to be a better, more authentic version of myself.

This book is dedicated to everyone who is on a journey to find themselves. My hope is that you connect to the essence of who you truly are.

Introduction

If you have chosen this book (or if it has chosen you), then you are probably in the process of searching for something – perhaps your sense of self, your purpose or the meaning of your life, or as a way to discover more about yourself and your relationships. In the current world where we are, more often than not, overstimulated and over busy, it can be a challenge to find opportunities to stop and reflect on how we are thinking and feeling, how we are choosing to live our lives and our relationships with the key people around us. Yet these factors have a profound influence on our quality of life and how we consciously or unconsciously choose to live. We may be pulled in lots of different emotional and practical directions, but let me ask you this question: if you don't invest in yourself, who will?

Fear and expectations (our own or other people's) can block us from being in touch with our true feelings and listening to our inner truth, causing us to feel disconnected from ourselves. In a world full of expectations, how do we learn to trust what feels right to us? We can be influenced to believe that we should live life in a certain way. This can be based on our family values, the parenting we received, the media that we consume, the influences around us, and our own beliefs or attitude. We refer to these influences as the conditions that have been placed on us which tell us who we should be and what life goals we should be aspiring to. This can dictate our thought processes and the decisions that we make. I will call this 'conditioned logic'. However, what if our conditioned logic and our heart's desires do not match up? Sometimes it's easier to follow the expectations that are thrust upon us. These are often the internalised 'shoulds' and 'musts', which become the conscious or unconscious rules that we live by. I will talk more about these later.

For now, let me pose this question to you: what if things could be different? What if we could live the life that we had always envisioned, with our inner and outer worlds aligned? What if we knew and believed that we are enough, just as we are? If your life could be any way that *you* desired, what would you be doing? How would you feel? What would you believe about yourself and others?

Following the recent turbulent years in particular, my belief is that we need to learn how to reflect rather than react. It is in this way that we can move from surviving to thriving. Stepping into our magic – our power – creates opportunities for transformation and change. This includes our mindset, emotions, reactions, values and relationship with ourselves and others. I have written this self-empowerment book for a couple of reasons. Firstly, I hope that you will utilise it as a tool to help you consciously pause and reflect. I want you to choose to experience and feel, rather than be told what to do, which only places another layer of conditioning on you. My hope is that you will take some time to invest in yourself – be it for the 30 days, or for whenever is the right time to take action for change. Whenever you feel ready, think of this book as a psychologist in your pocket who is there to support you in the process of reflecting on yourself and your life.

Secondly, I have always been fascinated by the power of relationships, which is probably why I became a psychologist. Relationships are the cornerstone of life and my aim is to help you explore the relationships in your life more deeply. At our core, we are relational beings. We learn the power of relationships as an instinctual part of our survival, so it is no wonder that relationships become a focus of our lives, whether consciously or unconsciously. Through our early attachments, we start to learn (rightly or wrongly) about how we perceive ourselves and the world around us. We can define ourselves and our world via our key relationships; this can either support or hinder us.

I want to be transparent and honest, so here is a reality check: change is a process and it takes time, consistency and persistence. This is not a 'quick fix' book. Real change takes dedication. You've likely picked up this book because you are curious, want to self-reflect and are open to change, which is a good start. You did not acquire your life patterns overnight and you can't expect them to change overnight, but with the right focus, it is possible to adjust these patterns and how you feel about yourself.

The focus of this book is self-empowerment, emphasising that *you* are in the driving seat of your life. It brings together almost two decades of my professional and life experiences in psychology, self-development and spiritual practices, which I have also harnessed for my own growth. As multifaceted beings, we are constantly presented with opportunities to grow and evolve, but it is up to us to take them. We can either stay stuck, or choose to change.

As you sit with various parts of yourself and explore aspects of your life, you will realise that the power to make changes that align with your authentic self lies within you *in the now*. Use this book in a way that makes sense to you. Come back to activities if you choose; take a break to digest things when necessary. Listen to yourself and trust the process of your journey. This book can also complement various forms of therapy, and you could use it as a journal and a way of checking in with yourself. It's your journey, take it at your own pace.

The process will be unique and individual to each person, but for all, it will be an ongoing process of evolution, progression and change. All that I ask is that you begin to trust yourself and the process. Are you ready to delve deeper?

1
Making This Book Work For You

Over the past seventeen years I have worked with people of all ages, from all walks of life. As a psychologist, many have come to me for support due to a conflict between their outer and inner worlds. On the surface they may appear to have it all – the job, success, relationship, appearance, fame or fortune – but beneath it, they are running away from themselves (including their thoughts and feelings) as they fundamentally feel, even after all this validation, that they are not good enough.

The term 'core belief' was coined by Beck to explain the deeply held assumptions that we have about ourselves or others (Beck, 1964). We can take these to be true, even if there is no real evidence for them, and we feel, think and act in accordance with our core beliefs. For some individuals, their core beliefs are centred around thoughts that they have failed in some way, or they may feel scared to fail. This can lead people to put unnecessary and unrealistic pressure on themselves. In this way, they spend their lives merely existing and going through the motions instead of living a truly authentic life where they are connected to their wants, needs, ambitions and desires. They are crippled, stuck and can feel guilty, ashamed or highly self-critical. They develop the false belief that doing more will help them to feel better, but rarely is this the case. In fact, this can often serve to solidify already unhealthy connections with themselves and the world around them.

You may assume that some people will have had it tougher than others, but I have come to learn that every person has their pain point. Often, it is linked to their self-image and associated beliefs. Sometimes, these beliefs can be limiting and can induce self-doubt, framed in words like 'I can't'. If limiting beliefs are not checked and challenged, it is easy for them to become a way of life. In this way, we make our limiting beliefs come true. Even if we appear successful by external standards, the internal workings of our mind can paint a different picture. This creates an internal conflict between what we are presenting to the world (usually based on what we think we 'should' be) and how we feel inside. This conflict can spread into our relationships and the roles that we take on in our lives. In this way, *fear* can drive us and our decisions. Shifting our mindset requires shifting our emotions and our self-perception. This is the way to elicit *real* change as, in order to change our mindset, we need to shift gears from reaction to reflection.

The need for self-reflection

It is at this point we welcome in the potentially scary notion of self-reflection. Sometimes we want it, but sometimes we do not. I often say that awareness is like a faulty light bulb – once it is switched on you may be able to dim it once in a while, but you won't be able to completely switch it off, no matter how hard you try. This may be an uncomfortable process to go through, but remaining stagnant, stuck and unhealed is uncomfortable too. We can get so used to running away from our feelings that we learn only how to avoid them or distract ourselves. But this does not mean that the feelings are not there. This just means that we lose our confidence in holding, understanding, processing, regulating and validating our emotions. In this way, over time, our feelings can become something to be feared, rather than leaned into.

Even when we feel that we are coping relatively well in life, we may be unconsciously repeating patterns that can block us from reaching our full potential. The first step is to create awareness of these patterns. This requires us to sit with some level of discomfort as we hold the metaphorical mirror up to ourselves and explore the ripple effects on our lives. The second step is to create empowered choice by asking the question: 'Am I ready to change?' Until you are ready – or until you are pushed into being ready – nothing changes.

The third step is to take action, as many times as is necessary, to get to a point of more contentment. This is not a linear process. It includes success, failure and readjustment. It is a process of turning the volume down on our internal worst enemies – self-doubt and self-criticism.

In this way, we can unlearn patterns and begin to create healthier ways of relating to ourselves and others, ways that are aligned with our authentic self. This unlearning and re-learning is empowerment. At times, it can be challenging and painful, but in order to find our true self, we need to go on a journey of self-discovery, to shed the layers of expectations that have been placed upon us.

Understanding the link between feelings, thoughts and behaviours

There is a connection between our feelings (emotional or physiological), thoughts (positive or negative) and behaviours (reactive or proactive), as shown in the image below.

As such, if we do not understand or are unable to regulate our emotions, or are overwhelmed by them, this can influence how we think. If we tend to have more negative thoughts (rather than balanced or positive thoughts), this is likely to increase the intensity of the emotions we are feeling at that point in time. In this

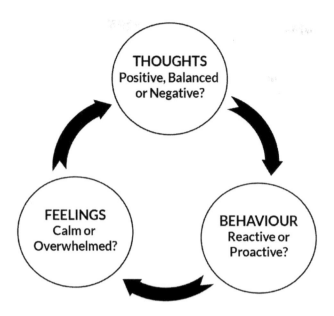

THE LINK BETWEEN FEELINGS, THOUGHTS AND BEHAVIOURS

instance, we may be more likely to behave in reactive or avoidant ways in order to help us try and manage the intensity of the emotion. This isn't always useful, as this cycle of behaviour can trigger a downward spiral into feeling more overwhelmed, with the number and intensity of negative thoughts increasing. If we understand ourselves in this way, we can see that how we feel, what we think and what we do are all interlinked.

By repeating the same cycle again and again, we create patterns around how we think, feel and respond to ourselves and the people and situations around us.

The good news is that once we become aware of this cycle, we have the opportunity to change it. Think about it as an old school vinyl record, playing on loop. Our bodies and brains get so used to being, thinking and reacting in the same way (we can create this cycle unconsciously and through habit), that it becomes our norm. The vinyl keeps playing the same song, even if it is not a song that we like.

The same is true of how we think about or relate to ourselves. We can choose to think and feel differently, and to react differently to our thoughts and feelings. When we have a sense of low worth or value, it is likely that we are feeling and thinking about ourselves in more negative ways. In this way, the behaviour that we choose may be disruptive or destructive rather than productive. When we bring this pattern to our relationships, it may cause us to choose the wrong relationships again and again or continue to internalise negative thoughts and self-talk, which ultimately makes us feel bad about ourselves.

But with awareness comes options. We can scratch the record up or choose to play a different song. To do this, we need to do two things. First, there needs to be an awareness that our feelings, thoughts, patterns and/or behaviours are not working for us. Second, we need to have a desire to consciously change and to choose new actions, thoughts and responses to emotions or behavioural patterns. Take a moment to identify your 'why'. Why do you want to know more about your internal processes? What would this give to you? You need to make these choices. No one else can do it for you.

This book will help you to start the process of listening to the vinyl playing in your head and identifying what song is playing to see if it's one you're happy with. Maybe you want to remix it, scratch it up or change the song completely. Herein lies the key – *you* are in control and *you choose* what changes you want to make and when. Going through this process will empower you to do what feels right for you in the now, not what you may have consciously or unconsciously internalised. You will learn to trust yourself and your needs, wants and desires.

Overview of the book

The activities in this book are divided into three main parts, all of which begin with an introduction to the section followed by daily practices designed to help you strengthen your connection to your true, authentic inner self, away from judgement and away from fear. If you can, try and read each daily activity in the morning before you get busy with your day. My suggestion would be to get into the habit of setting aside ten minutes at roughly the same time each day for the daily activity.

The first section, **My Internal World**, is focused on the relationship you have with yourself. The second section, **My External World**, is focused on your outer world and the key relationships around you. The third section, **My True Self**, helps you to connect with who you really are and your needs, wants and desires. This section will help you to blend the learning that you gain from sections one and two with the aim of helping you shift to living a more authentic life in the now. This will take you closer to action steps, thoughts and feelings that align with your ideal self.

Are you ready to discover who you are in the here and now, and to step back into your position of power? This journey may not be easy, but it will be worth it. As you have picked up this book, on some level you have already recognised that you are worth investing in. Sometimes, our investment in ourselves can be overshadowed by the thoughts, values and beliefs imposed on us by ourselves, others, or a combination of the two. We may feel we need to adhere to these, even if they do not feel quite right. As you work though this book, you will learn more about the role that you have been playing in defining yourself and where your power currently lies. This will help you to identify what changes you may need to make and what feels right for you.

Remember that you are a work in progress, so be kind to yourself. When we go through any change, it can bring up challenging emotions and we may feel that we are not making much progress, but I encourage you to persevere – speak to a friend, family member or professional if you need to. Toward the end of the book I provide a list of services and sources available in the UK, should you need them. Get ready to step into this journey of self-discovery and tap into the power of yourself, for *you* are the magic.

How to use this book

My hope is that this book will keep you focused and give you some space to reflect. Reflecting is one thing, but in order to elicit change, we need to *take action*. As such, the book contains a series of activities designed to help you actively work on yourself and your relationships by challenging your thoughts, perceived limitations and behaviours and connecting you with your emotions. Some changes and reflections might feel easier than others.

You choose how to make this book work for you. You can work through the book in a chronological order from Day 1 to Day 30, or dip into it and pick one activity to focus on at a time.

This book has been designed with a journal-style format, outlining the activity of the day and then giving you space to reflect. There is a journaling space after each daily activity which is optional, but encouraged as it will help strengthen your inner voice. The journal section provides some tools and questions that you can use to reflect on the activity and what you have learned. This will also help you to identify any potential actions you have taken, or would like to take. If you are accessing the e-book version, I would suggest making notes in a physical journal, on a tablet, computer or even your phone. You could also audio record any thoughts and experiences for you to reflect on.

☆ DAY XXX ☆ ACTIVITY OF THE DAY

DAILY REFLECTIVE JOURNAL 📅

My chosen affirmation for the day:

Pre-activity check-in

Mark the strength of your feelings today on the scale below.

(1) (2) (3) (4) (5) (6) (7) (8) (9) (10)

(weak)   (strong)

What is my mood and the strength of this mood?

> What are my main thoughts and the strength of these thoughts?

Post-activity check-in

Mark the strength of your feelings today on the scale below.

(1) (2) (3) (4) (5) (6) (7) (8) (9) (10)
(weak)   (strong)

> What is my mood and the strength of this mood?

> What are my main thoughts and the strength of these thoughts?

> **Reflections:** How did this activity/today impact on me?

> **Learning:** What did I learn about myself or my relationships today?

How will I apply this learning and/or take action?

What am I grateful for (internally or externally)?

Is there anything that I need to do in order to take care of myself today?

Did I use any positive coping strategies today?

Affirmations

You will notice that each daily reflective journal page has a 'chosen affirmation for the day' section. Affirmations can be useful in helping to shift our mindset over time, so that we skew it away from negative thinking patterns and toward the positive. There is evidence that we can alter the neural pathways in our brain through regular practices that help us to balance our thoughts and engrain more positive thinking patterns (Bloch, 2015; Hölzel et al, 2010, 2011; Poerio et al, 2017). When practised consistently, positivity is more likely to become our default mindset. The more you practise, the greater the shift. Over time, small steps create bigger shifts, helping to reset our mind and thoughts to work for us rather than against us. Consistency is key.

Affirmations can either be about yourself and linked to your values as a person (eg, 'I am' statements) or they can be about the world around you (eg, 'Many opportunities await me'). It is important to note that this process is much more than simply being more positive. For example, if I am internally saying to myself daily, 'I am awful and I mess everything up,' then simply repeating 'I am amazing' several times a day (when I don't *feel* this way) will not change my internal self-talk. This is because I am not connecting to the new statement on an emotional level, so I am probably not thinking and acting in a way that aligns to the statement

'I am amazing'. Therefore, it would be better to start with a statement that was more believable for me in relation to where I was on my journey. Such an example could be 'I may not be perfect, but I am improving every day'.

The affirmations are not pre-selected for you. You can choose whether to use them or not and you can choose affirmations that feel right for you. They do not always have to be positive if this does not feel genuine. They can also be more neutral (eg, 'I am capable of dealing with any challenges that come my way'). The key thing about affirmations is that not only do you say them, but you also need to feel them. If your affirmation were true, how would this impact on you? You need to visualise yourself in that scenario: how would you be thinking and feeling and what would you be doing? Over time, this gets you used to feeling, thinking and acting in this more idealised and positive way, so that your mind begins to naturally focus on how you can create more of those feelings and actions in the now.

I have included some affirmation cards at the end of this book for inspiration, but you should create your own. It is not just about saying the words, the main thing is that you *connect* to the words and feelings. If you do not feel ready to use the affirmations at first, that is fine. If you do decide to use them, come back to your chosen affirmation regularly throughout the day. You can write it down, say it out loud, voice record it and play it back to yourself daily, or visualise images or places associated with it.

Before you start: Check-in and personal goals

Sometimes, it is hard to recognise just how far we have come. To help with this, I have developed a quick check-in tool that you can utilise at the beginning and end of this book, to track the progress you make on your 30-day journey. This can also help to identify the areas of your life where you may need some extra support or where you could be kinder to yourself. It also creates an opportunity to think about your longer-term emotional goals, while giving you a snapshot of where you are at the moment.

Rate yourself on the following statements (where 1 is low and 10 is high):

I am happy.

(1) (2) (3) (4) (5) (6) (7) (8) (9) (10)
(weak)   (strong)

I am confident.

(1) (2) (3) (4) (5) (6) (7) (8) (9) (10)
(weak)   (strong)

I am of value.

(1) (2) (3) (4) (5) (6) (7) (8) (9) (10)

(weak)   (strong)

I am content.

(1) (2) (3) (4) (5) (6) (7) (8) (9) (10)

(weak)   (strong)

My life is balanced.

(1) (2) (3) (4) (5) (6) (7) (8) (9) (10)

(weak)   (strong)

I listen to my needs.

(1) (2) (3) (4) (5) (6) (7) (8) (9) (10)

(weak)   (strong)

I am able to say no when I need to.

(1) (2) (3) (4) (5) (6) (7) (8) (9) (10)

(weak)   (strong)

I feel secure in my life.

(1) (2) (3) (4) (5) (6) (7) (8) (9) (10)

(weak)   (strong)

The vinyl wheel

Use the 'vinyl' wheel template below to plot out how satisfied you are with different areas of your life (with 10 being 'very satisfied' and 0 being 'not satisfied'). Use a coloured pencil to mark where you think you are on each of the areas. This will give you an overall, holistic view of your life now and will help you to identify whether certain areas need to be explored further or prioritised.

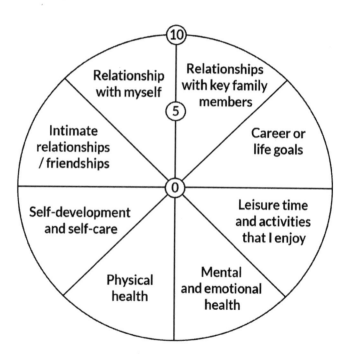

Any reflections on my scales and/or vinyl wheel:

Looking at the above, I would like to make the following changes in my life (try and identify specific personal goals):

I would like to make these changes because:

The goal/area of my life that I will start with is:

My commitment to myself

I want you to get the most from this book – not for me, but for you. To do this, it is useful to make a commitment to yourself. How will you use the activities in this book? How often? How much time will you spend on yourself each day? How will you prioritise yourself when life gets in the way? How will you persevere?

Take a moment to consider these questions. When we reflect, we can then put in place strategies and a plan. This makes us more likely to continue forming and solidifying positive habits over time. Committing to the 30 days outlined in this book is a good place to start. Having a plan in place also makes it more likely that you can overcome any worst-case scenarios or challenge any procrastination or excuses that you may be likely to make in the next 30 days. The following questions will help you to think about how you will commit to your self-growth.

My hopes for engaging with this book are:

I will commit to my self-growth by:

I will prioritise my needs, even when life gets busy, by:

I will practise self-care by:

I will show myself that I am worthy by:

It is important for me to make these changes in my life because:

Trigger warning: if you have had difficulty with attachment or trauma, please pace yourself. You may wish to refer to the mindfulness and grounding techniques and helpful links list included in this book, as well as your support networks, should you feel emotionally triggered.

2

My Internal World
(Days 1–11)

This first section, about your **internal world**, is focused on the relationship that you have with yourself in the now. This can be heavily influenced by the attachments in your key relationships. This chapter aims to connect you to your inner world and early conditioning, some of which you may be aware of and some of which may be unconsciously driving you. Are you ready to go inward?

What is attachment and why does it matter?

As babies, we attach to our primary caregiver(s), which can be parents, guardians, carers, siblings, extended family members and so on. It is the person or people who had the responsibility for taking care of your practical and emotional needs. This first attachment forms the basis of what we learn about relationships, including how we trust, what makes us feel safe and secure, our perception of the world and the people in it and how we react or behave in certain situations. It influences what we internalise about the world and ourselves, and this internal model determines how we view the world, whether we see it as safe or unsafe. It also impacts our levels of self-esteem and self-worth, as we internalise what value we have, based on how the early attachment figure(s) have responded to our physical, mental and emotional needs.

If our initial early relationships were often unpredictable, unstable or unsafe, this affects the way that we interact with other key people later in our lives. These early relationships form the blueprint for our future relationships. Although we can change these patterns, it is important to recognise that our interaction(s) with our primary caregiver(s) as a child set the tone for the attachment patterns in significant relationships throughout our lives. On an unconscious level, we may seek relationships that recreate familiar patterns. This isn't about logic; it is about our primitive survival instinct. Yet it has the potential to lead us into relationships that may be unhealthy, or harmful to our emotional, mental or physical wellbeing. It is important to state here that we are all individual and this does not necessarily apply to everyone who has experienced unpredictable or unsafe early attachments. Yet these individuals may find themselves impacted in different ways, for example being less trusting, wary of others or less likely to emotionally invest in relationships, depending on the coping mechanisms that they employed as children, which they may also utilise as adults.

Delving into complex trauma is beyond the scope of this book, but it is important to acknowledge it. Difficult, frightening or stressful life experiences, such as loss and abuse, can impact how safe we feel in the world. Trauma can result from being directly harmed or placed in direct danger, witnessing harm to someone else, living in a frightening or unpredictable environment, or being exposed to someone else's trauma or a community affected by trauma – from a one-off incident or a series of events. Trauma can happen at any age, to anyone, and everyone will respond to it in a unique way. The impact it has will depend on previous experiences of trauma, the number and intensity of life stressors experienced, the nature of the trauma, how many safe relationships are present and if the person feels supported and validated at the time or after the incident. Abuse can be violent or nonviolent and it can include sexual, financial, emotional, psychological and physical abuse. **If you would like to access more information about abuse, please refer to the Additional Resources section where you will find a list of useful resources and helpline numbers.**

Understanding survival mode

It is likely that anyone who has experienced these concerns has become used to being in 'survival mode' as a way of coping. In a nutshell, we usually go into survival mode, 'fight or flight', when we feel in emotional or physical danger. When considering safety, it is important to consider psychological safety too. For example, someone may have their physical needs met, but still experience emotional neglect or feel that their emotions were not validated, that love was conditional or they were not seen, heard or understood by their primary caregiver(s).

The fight or flight response is linked to the release of cortisol (the 'stress hormone') and adrenaline, which is the body's natural way of preparing to cope with danger. It is an automatic response to danger linked to the primitive brain, meaning the body at that point cannot tell the difference between real or perceived danger, or between physical and emotional threat. We usually respond to danger in one of four ways:

1. **Fight:** This is where we protest, struggle or fight back against the danger. It can be linked to anger and irritability.

2. **Flight:** This can be seen as running away or hiding from the danger. It can be linked to avoidance of people, situations or emotions.

3. **Freeze:** This is an experience of numbness or being cut off from the situation or emotion being experienced.

4. **Fawn:** This can include trying to appease, please or pacify the source of the harm (eg, a particular person).

All of the above are protective mechanisms. All of them are also automatic, part of our survival instinct. Trauma can leave you feeling frightened, invalidated, under threat, humiliated, rejected, abandoned, unsafe, unsupported, trapped, ashamed or powerless. These feelings can be triggering in the now, which may make it more challenging to separate the past from the present and cause those affected to feel emotions more intensely, or to be hypervigilant or on edge.

When we go into a state of surviving rather than thriving, this triggers our primitive brain as we feel emotionally overwhelmed (eg, feelings of fear or anxiety). In order to survive the perceived threat, our primitive brain then hijacks the logical brain (prefrontal cortex) and we become less able to regulate our emotions or make logical decisions, until we start to feel emotionally and/ or physically safe again (Shalev et al, 1996; Van Der Kolk et al, 1996; Saigh and Bremner, 1999; Casey et al, 2000). It can also impact on how we behave, as when we are in survival mode we may be more impulsive, overwhelmed or feel vulnerable. We may go out of our way to not make ourselves emotionally vulnerable, for example by avoiding conflict, having a lack of empathy for others or shutting ourselves off from our feelings. But in the absence of real danger, the more we avoid feeling fearful or anxious, the more intense the anxiety and fear becomes as we don't give ourselves the opportunity to challenge our assumption that we are unsafe or that we can't cope. If we are constantly in survival mode, this also impacts on how much we emotionally connect with others, as we may not have the energy or focus to do so, or feel too scared.

The good news is it's never too late to change things. This is highlighted in the concept of neuroplasticity. Consistent, physically and emotionally safe and healthy relationships can create new neural pathways in the brain as the brain is able to adapt and change in line with our experiences and learning from them. This re-wires the brain over time and can take us out of survival mode. Our brains can evolve in accordance with our experiences *today*, rather than those in the past (Kaczmarek, 2020; Chen et al, 2020; Tahmasian et al, 2020).

What are the different attachment styles?

In general terms, attachment is the foundation for how you relate to others, a blueprint for life that is established in our early relationships. We learn about ourselves, others and the world based on how our caregiver(s) related to us as babies and throughout our childhood. This determines how we relate to friends, family and romantic relationships in adulthood. Once you identify your attachment style, you can begin to consciously make changes (if you would like to).

Attachment theory was developed through the work of John Bowlby in the 1950s and Mary Ainsworth in the 1970s (Bowlby, 1969; Ainsworth et al, 1978). Bowlby worked with children and parents to explore the parent–child relationship. He studied parents' responses to their child, looking at whether their relating was appropriate and sensitive, effective, safe, secure and loving. Today, there are four main widely accepted parent–child attachment styles which came out of the work of Ainsworth and Main and Solomon (Ainsworth et al, 1978; Main & Solomon, 1986):

★ **Secure.** The child was responded to appropriately by their main caregiver(s) and their emotional needs were met. In adulthood, they are generally trusting of others and relationships feel relatively safe emotionally.

★ **Insecure: Anxious avoidant.** This can develop when the main caregiver(s) were emotionally or physically absent. It can create an internal narrative of 'I am on my own' or a sense of the child feeling rejected. Children with this experience usually learn to become independent and can avoid their caregivers as a source of comfort. As adults, these children may not ask for help, avoid situations that make them anxious (so don't take many risks) and might find it difficult to trust others.

★ **Insecure: Anxious ambivalent.** This can be described as a 'push and pull' dynamic where the child oscillates from being clingy to pushing caregiver(s) away. They may not have felt comforted by their caregiver(s) or may have rejected them. As adults, these children may fear rejection, have a fear of abandonment, feel overly jealous or not easily trust others.

★ **Insecure: Anxious disorganised.** This style can develop when there was an ongoing lack of consistency in the actions and behaviours of the caregiver(s), leading to confusion. These children show a lack of clear attachment behaviour and their responses to their caregivers are constantly changing eg, avoidance or resistance. As adults, they can find it hard to understand and regulate their emotions – at times, they may feel cut off from their emotions and at other times overwhelmed by them. Relationships might feel emotionally unsafe or confusing to navigate.

QUIZ: WHAT IS YOUR ATTACHMENT STYLE IN RELATIONSHIPS?

Read through the following statements and mark 'yes' or 'no' for each of them. Do not overthink it, go with the answer that instinctually feels right. Each sentence will have a letter attached to it. At the end of the quiz, count up your responses to identify your most common letter and check the corresponding attachment style. This may give you some indication of your attachment style. It is important to say that the purpose of this quiz is not to assess or define you, or pass judgement, but to give you some indication of the characteristics that you *may* bring to your current relationships. It is worth reflecting on all the questions and reading through each of the attachment styles at the end to see what resonates most strongly with you. Remember, no one fits into a neat category and *you* are the expert on yourself. You may find that different attachment styles are present in different relationships that have varying levels of emotional risk attached to them.

★ I find it easy to trust others (A) yes/no

★ When in a relationship, I worry that my partner doesn't love me (B) yes/no

★ I find it difficult to share my feelings and/or thoughts with my partner (C) yes/no

★ I struggle to directly communicate my needs to my partner (D) yes/no

★ I am comfortable sharing my needs with my partner (A) yes/no

★ I am extremely distressed when a relationship ends (B) yes/no

★ I find it challenging to be emotionally intimate in a relationship (C) yes/no

★ I would be described as oversensitive (D) yes/no

★ I am able to soothe and support my partner when they are distressed (A) yes/no

★ I resist getting close to people (B) yes/no

★ I often downplay the importance of relationships in my life (C) yes/no

★ I feel comfortable and frightened at the same time in relationships (D) yes/no

★ I am able to ask for appropriate support when I need it (A) yes/no

★ I fear rejection (B) yes/no

★ I keep my emotions to myself (C) yes/no

★ I tend to play the role of caregiver/parent in relationships (D) yes/no

★ I am able to handle conflict (A) yes/no

★ I find myself being clingy in relationships (B) yes/no

★ I find it hard to ask for what I need (C) yes/no

★ I am highly anxious in relationships (D) yes/no

★ I am able to regulate my moods (A) yes/no

★ I become jealous easily (B) yes/no

★ Other people's opinions of my relationship are important (C) yes/no

★ I don't always feel in control of my relationships (D) yes/no

★ In general, I feel good about myself (A) yes/no

★ I push others away before they hurt me (B) yes/no

★ I find it hard to be emotionally vulnerable in relationships (C) yes/no

★ I find it hard to trust others (D) yes/no

Secure attachment: mostly As

As adults, these people usually:

★ Are trusting of others

★ Are able to choose to stay in lasting relationships

★ Feel good about themselves in general and have high self-esteem

★ Are comfortable sharing their feelings with partners and friends

★ Can seek out social support and support others in balance

★ Communicate openly and honestly

★ Are independent but still able to emotionally connect to others

Ambivalent attachment: mostly Bs

As adults, these individuals may present the following behaviours:

- ★ Reluctance to get emotionally close to others
- ★ Worry about what others think about them
- ★ Worry that they are unlovable
- ★ Find the end of relationships distressing
- ★ Dependence in relationships
- ★ Feel highly anxious in relationships or fear rejection
- ★ Question their worth or value

Avoidant attachment: mostly Cs

As adults, these individuals may:

- ★ Appear to be self-reliant
- ★ Find it hard to emotionally invest in relationships
- ★ Minimise the importance of the relationships in their lives
- ★ Find intimacy challenging
- ★ Expect relationships to end

Disorganised attachment: mostly Ds

As adults, these individuals may:

- ★ Find relationships confusing
- ★ Feel emotionally triggered in relationships and not have the words to express themselves, so do this through actions instead

★ Be nervous or apprehensive in relationships or appear 'overly sensitive'

★ Take on a parental role in relationships

For us to change the way we relate to others, we first need to have an awareness of where we're at. I hope that the above quiz and answers have given you some insight into your potential attachment style and the ways that you may relate to others. The daily activities in this section will help you to continue to gain more insight. Remember to be patient with yourself as you transform – change is a process and it can take some time to shift old patterns of behaviour and embed new learning.

Even if you perceive your attachment style to be secure, reflecting on your internal world can be a useful way of fine-tuning the unconscious mind to prepare you for future relationships, connections, friendships and intimate relationships and for re-engaging with current ones. It can also help you to understand and reflect on other people's attachment style and what their behaviour may be signalling to you. This chapter will provide you with some mechanisms for coping with emotionally challenging relationships, should you need them.

☆ DAY 1 ☆ BODY SCAN

ACTIVITY OF THE DAY

As previously mentioned, there is a link between feelings, thoughts and behaviours. In mindfulness techniques, we focus on the here and now. We remain curious about our experiences, without feeling the need to judge or change our state or thoughts. We are in tune with who we are and what we are feeling in the moment. We imagine that our awareness is like a light that we are brightening as we continue with our mindfulness-based journey in this chapter. Today's activity will focus on helping us to become more mindful and focused on the present moment, with the aim of remaining curious about and nonjudgemental of our thoughts or feelings. This is crucial for building a healthier relationship with ourselves, allowing all parts of us to be heard and validated. Over time, this can reduce self-criticism.

Below is a script for a body scan exercise. This is a way to attune to what you are feeling or experiencing and to 'check in' with yourself. Read through this script before trying the activity. You can also listen to an audio version of this via my website or record your own version to listen to.

Body scan exercise

1. Sit in a comfortable position and close your eyes if this feels comfortable, or lower your gaze.

2. Take three breaths in and out. Check in with your body, noticing any sensations and feeling contact with the floor.

3. Now start scanning your body and noticing the different parts. You are not going to judge what you are thinking or feeling, just be still and notice it.

   - To start with, pay attention to your face and head. Can you feel anything here (eg, tingling, numbness, tightness, warmth, coldness)? Do you notice anything in your mind? Is your face relaxed or scrunched up? How do the various features on your face feel – your eyes, nose, mouth? Can you hear or smell anything?

   - Now move your attention to the neck and shoulders. How do they feel?

   - Now move into your upper arms. Do they feel heavy or relaxed? Are your hands hot or cold?

4. Take one more deep breath and pay attention to your whole body. What does it feel like? How do you feel when you breathe in and out?

5. Take a final deep breath in and out. When you are ready, open your eyes and come back into the room.

DAILY REFLECTIVE JOURNAL

My chosen affirmation for the day:

Pre-activity check-in

Mark the strength of your feelings today on the scale below.

(1) (2) (3) (4) (5) (6) (7) (8) (9) (10)
(weak)   (strong)

What is my mood and the strength of this mood?

What are my main thoughts and the strength of these thoughts?

Post-activity check-in

Mark the strength of your feelings today on the scale below.

(1) (2) (3) (4) (5) (6) (7) (8) (9) (10)
(weak)   (strong)

What is my mood and the strength of this mood?

What are my main thoughts and the strength of these thoughts?

Reflections: How did this activity/today impact on me?

Learning: What did I learn about myself or my relationships today?

How will I apply this learning and/or take action?

What am I grateful for (internally or externally)?

Is there anything that I need to do in order to take care of myself today?

Did I use any positive coping strategies today?

☆ DAY 2 ☆ EMOTIONAL REGULATION

ACTIVITY OF THE DAY

It is important we understand how to regulate our emotions so that we feel calmer, more relaxed and able to thoughtfully challenge and deal with situations in an appropriate manner. Our bodies cannot be physiologically stressed and relaxed at the same time, so by altering the physical state in our bodies, we alter how we think and respond to the situation that we are in. Grounding techniques can be useful strategies to utilise when you need to feel more centred and present in the moment. Think of them as a set of tools that you can utilise as and when you need to.

Like any skill, grounding techniques take practice; the more you practise them, the easier and more familiar they will become. I would encourage you to practise these techniques when you are in a calm and relaxed state; this will make them easier to apply in situations where you feel stressed, anxious or overwhelmed. Below are some examples of techniques that can help us to do this; they are good to use when we feel anxious, stressed, frustrated or overwhelmed, or if we simply want to feel calmer and more relaxed. Today, choose one of these techniques to practise.

Deep breathing

The basis of any relaxation or grounding techniques is deep breathing. This means taking slower, deeper breaths and paying more attention to the way that you breathe. When we are stressed or anxious, our breathing becomes faster and more irregular; we may even hold our breath. This is a simple thing to alter.

To practise deep breathing, start by sitting or standing comfortably and keep your back relatively straight. I always encourage people to take their awareness to their feet on the floor so that they feel grounded. Try to have your shoulders pushed back slightly (but not to the point that you are uncomfortable) to open up your chest area. Notice and pay attention to your breath. Now breathe in through your nose and out through your mouth and continue until you are in a slow and steady rhythm. If you like, you can count in your head to help keep a steady pace. For example, breathing in for one... two... and breathing out for one... two... or saying to yourself in your mind 'I am breathing in for one, I am breathing out for one,' 'I am breathing in for two, I am breathing out for two,' and so on until you get to ten breaths. You could also imagine breathing in a colour of your choice and imagine it flowing through your body as you breathe in and out. Choose a colour that makes you feel calm and relaxed, or a colour that you like.

Square breathing

This is a variation of the deep breathing technique above. To help you, you can draw a square, look at a square object, trace a square on your leg as you go through the technique or imagine a square in your mind. In this technique, you breathe in (through your nose), hold the breath (so that your stomach expands), breathe out (through your mouth) and hold (your stomach may feel empty). It can take a few goes to get into a rhythm but you will soon find a flow. Remembering the instructions helps you to stay focused and present in the moment. If you like, you can also attach a count to help slow your breathing down, for example, 'Breathe in for one... two... hold for one... two... breathe out for one... two... and hold for one... two...' You should continue to go through the square breathing for at least a few rounds or until you feel calmer and more relaxed.

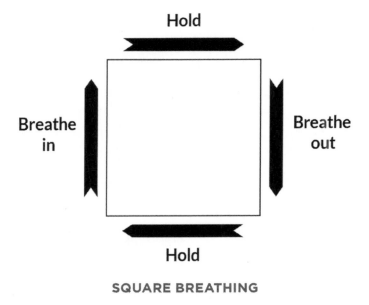

SQUARE BREATHING

DAILY REFLECTIVE JOURNAL

My chosen affirmation for the day:

Pre-activity check-in

Mark the strength of your feelings today on the scale below.

(1) (2) (3) (4) (5) (6) (7) (8) (9) (10)

(weak)   (strong)

What is my mood and the strength of this mood?

What are my main thoughts and the strength of these thoughts?

Post-activity check-in

Mark the strength of your feelings today on the scale below.

(1) (2) (3) (4) (5) (6) (7) (8) (9) (10)

(weak)   (strong)

What is my mood and the strength of this mood?

What are my main thoughts and the strength of these thoughts?

Reflections: How did this activity/today impact on me?

Learning: What did I learn about myself or my relationships today?

How will I apply this learning and/or take action?

What am I grateful for (internally or externally)?

Is there anything that I need to do in order to take care of myself today?

Did I use any positive coping strategies today?

☆ DAY 3 ☆   PRESS THE PAUSE BUTTON

ACTIVITY OF THE DAY

This is a great method to use when you feel like your emotions may be taking over and you are less able to respond with your thinking brain. It goes like this:

1. If you are in a situation that is triggering you or increasing your emotional overwhelm, imagine pressing a pause button on the situation.

2. Check in with how your body is feeling. What sensations do you notice and where in your body do you feel them?

3. Now, detach from the situation by zooming out. You could imagine that you are looking at yourself in the situation from a distance.

4. Take a breath and ask yourself, 'How am I feeling and what do I need right now?' Write down any self-care or problem-solving strategies that come to mind.

5. Take another breath and ease back into your day when you are ready.

DAILY REFLECTIVE JOURNAL

My chosen affirmation for the day:

Pre-activity check-in

Mark the strength of your feelings today on the scale below.

(1) (2) (3) (4) (5) (6) (7) (8) (9) (10)
(weak)   (strong)

What is my mood and the strength of this mood?

What are my main thoughts and the strength of these thoughts?

Post-activity check-in

Mark the strength of your feelings today on the scale below.

(1) (2) (3) (4) (5) (6) (7) (8) (9) (10)
(weak)   (strong)

What is my mood and the strength of this mood?

What are my main thoughts and the strength of these thoughts?

Reflections: How did this activity/today impact on me?

Learning: What did I learn about myself or my relationships today?

How will I apply this learning and/or take action?

What am I grateful for (internally or externally)?

Is there anything that I need to do in order to take care of myself today?

Did I use any positive coping strategies today?

☆ DAY 4 ☆ RETRAIN YOUR BRAIN

ACTIVITY OF THE DAY

This is another emotional regulation technique that you may find useful in changing your perspective to a more positive one over time. Spend ten minutes on this activity.

1. Write a list of a few times you have felt joy. Connect to this feeling and notice what joy feels like in your body.

2. Now reflect on the positive things in your life at this moment in time and write down three things you are grateful for. Do this daily if you can.

3. Choose to do an activity today that brings you joy, no matter how big or small it is – for example having a coffee, going for a walk or speaking to a loved one.

4. If you find yourself worrying about life or feeling stuck then:

    -   Reflect on times that you have overcome challenges

    -   Consider what this says about your strengths? Eg, 'I am resilient'

    -   Make a plan for dealing with the worst-case scenario (even if this is not the most realistic case)

DAILY REFLECTIVE JOURNAL

My chosen affirmation for the day:

Pre-activity check-in

Mark the strength of your feelings today on the scale below.

(1) (2) (3) (4) (5) (6) (7) (8) (9) (10)
(weak)   (strong)

What is my mood and the strength of this mood?

What are my main thoughts and the strength of these thoughts?

Post-activity check-in

Mark the strength of your feelings today on the scale below.

(1) (2) (3) (4) (5) (6) (7) (8) (9) (10)
(weak)   (strong)

What is my mood and the strength of this mood?

What are my main thoughts and the strength of these thoughts?

Reflections: How did this activity/today impact on me?

Learning: What did I learn about myself or my relationships today?

How will I apply this learning and/or take action?

What am I grateful for (internally or externally)?

Is there anything that I need to do in order to take care of myself today?

Did I use any positive coping strategies today?

☆ DAY 5 ☆ TURN THE TIMER ON

ACTIVITY OF THE DAY

Today's activity requires you to set aside some time for a couple of minutes of grounding reflection with a positive, practical focus that should leave you feeling empowered and energised.

1. Sit with your thoughts. Put a timer on for two minutes and acknowledge your emotions and thoughts, anything that surfaces. Write them down.

2. Then, spend five minutes reflecting on and writing down what things are within your control.

3. Based on this, next write down what action steps you can take to feel more empowered.

4. Ground yourself by looking around your space and noticing three things that you can see.

5. For the rest of the day, honour yourself by fully engaging in what you are doing with all your senses. Focus on one task at a time.

DAILY REFLECTIVE JOURNAL

My chosen affirmation for the day:

Pre-activity check-in

Mark the strength of your feelings today on the scale below.

(1) (2) (3) (4) (5) (6) (7) (8) (9) (10)
(weak)   (strong)

What is my mood and the strength of this mood?

What are my main thoughts and the strength of these thoughts?

Post-activity check-in

Mark the strength of your feelings today on the scale below.

(1) (2) (3) (4) (5) (6) (7) (8) (9) (10)
(weak)   (strong)

What is my mood and the strength of this mood?

What are my main thoughts and the strength of these thoughts?

Reflections: How did this activity/today impact on me?

Learning: What did I learn about myself or my relationships today?

How will I apply this learning and/or take action?

What am I grateful for (internally or externally)?

Is there anything that I need to do in order to take care of myself today?

Did I use any positive coping strategies today?

☆ DAY 6 ☆   TURN DOWN THE CRITICAL VOICE

ACTIVITY OF THE DAY

Do you have a critical voice inside of your head? If yes, then how loud is it? Self-criticism is not kind, compassionate, loving or caring and it does nothing for how we feel about ourselves, including our levels of self-esteem and self-worth. It makes us feel weak, rather than empowered.

Today, your task is to notice and pay close attention to your thoughts. Spend ten minutes noticing any self-critical thoughts and ideally write them down. This process of bringing our thoughts to our conscious awareness is extremely important. Over time, it helps us to change the voice in our head.

When you notice a negative or self-critical thought, reflect on this thought. Is it a fact, fear or an opinion? Before you identify it as a fact, stop to look for evidence that says this thought is 100% true. That there is no doubt about it. That it would stand up in court. If you cannot say that it's 100% true, it's not a fact. It could fall into the 'opinion' or 'fear' categories, both of which can be changed. Opinions may be our own or other peoples, and they are not necessarily true, even if it may feel this way.

Noting down your thoughts in this way helps you to ascertain whether your self-talk is more positive or negative. Reflecting on your negative thoughts helps you to decide whether to keep, challenge or change them to more balanced thoughts. Confronting your critical thoughts also takes their power away.

Now create an alternative statement, based on a more self-loving voice. This voice could be inspired by the people who love, value and care for you; or, you could think about how you would speak to someone that you love and care for. It can be your own voice, an imagined voice, the voice of someone who inspires you or the voice of someone who makes you feel safe. See that voice as having control of the volume dial and use your alternative statement when you notice that your critical voice is a bit too loud.

Below, I have included a template that you could use to map out this process visually to make it easier to re-flect on both the self-critical and the self-loving voices.

Critical Thought	Fact, Fear or Opinion?	Alternative, Loving Statement

DAILY REFLECTIVE JOURNAL

My chosen affirmation for the day:

Pre-activity check-in

Mark the strength of your feelings today on the scale below.

(1) (2) (3) (4) (5) (6) (7) (8) (9) (10)
(weak)   (strong)

What is my mood and the strength of this mood?

What are my main thoughts and the strength of these thoughts?

Post-activity check-in

Mark the strength of your feelings today on the scale below.

(1) (2) (3) (4) (5) (6) (7) (8) (9) (10)
(weak)   (strong)

What is my mood and the strength of this mood?

What are my main thoughts and the strength of these thoughts?

Reflections: How did this activity/today impact on me?

Learning: What did I learn about myself or my relationships today?

How will I apply this learning and/or take action?

What am I grateful for (internally or externally)?

Is there anything that I need to do in order to take care of myself today?

Did I use any positive coping strategies today?

☆ DAY 7 ☆ CHALLENGING SELF-SABOTAGE

ACTIVITY OF THE DAY

When we undermine or undervalue ourselves, this is self-sabotage. This may lead us to engage in behaviours that are emotionally, mentally, spiritually or physically unhealthy, and to view ourselves and our capabilities in a limited way.

Today's task is to pay attention to the following:

1. How often you use self-defeating or disempowering statements like 'I can't', 'I should', 'I must', 'I have to'. Note all these instances down. These statements suggest that you may hold limiting beliefs, either about yourself or your world. Leading on from yesterday's activity, try and find a more compassionate voice.

2. Write all of the statements down (see below) and, at the end of the day, reflect on them, asking:

    -   What do they say about how you are treating yourself now and the limits that you are placing on yourself?

    -   Is there anything that you would like to change?

CHALLENGING SELF-SABOTAGE

Trigger	Self-defeating statement	Comparisons	Strategy for staying on track with healthy habits and goals
Person, place, situation, time of day etc – what led you to feel more emotionally vulnerable in that moment?	Eg, 'I can't do this.'	Eg, 'everyone else is better than me.'	Eg, have social media-free time, engage in a grounding technique, do something fun, set yourself a small challenge, reflect on your strengths, etc.

DAILY REFLECTIVE JOURNAL

My chosen affirmation for the day:

Pre-activity check-in

Mark the strength of your feelings today on the scale below.

(1) (2) (3) (4) (5) (6) (7) (8) (9) (10)

(weak)   (strong)

What is my mood and the strength of this mood?

What are my main thoughts and the strength of these thoughts?

Post-activity check-in

Mark the strength of your feelings today on the scale below.

(1) (2) (3) (4) (5) (6) (7) (8) (9) (10)

(weak)   (strong)

What is my mood and the strength of this mood?

What are my main thoughts and the strength of these thoughts?

Reflections: How did this activity/today impact on me?

Learning: What did I learn about myself or my relationships today?

How will I apply this learning and/or take action?

What am I grateful for (internally or externally)?

Is there anything that I need to do in order to take care of myself today?

Did I use any positive coping strategies today?

☆ DAY 8 ☆ THE MEANING OF LOVE

ACTIVITY OF THE DAY

We all have internalised beliefs about love – some are conscious and some are less obvious. We internalise these beliefs as a result of our life experiences. Early childhood experiences are particularly important – as mentioned earlier, these can influence the relationships we form and the type of love that we seek out.

Today's activity asks you to reflect on your definition of love. You can use these reflections to check in on yourself and the relationships around you as well as to help you seek out and communicate what it is that you need. Do this by spending ten minutes answering the following questions – see if anything surprises you:

★ When I hear the word 'love', the feelings and thoughts that come up for me are...

★ The positives of love are...

★ The negatives of love are...

★ What I need to feel safe in love is...

Now consciously re-define what love means to you, making it something that empowers and validates you.

★ **The version of love that I choose is...**
   (write down a word, a series of words or a short sentence)

DAILY REFLECTIVE JOURNAL

My chosen affirmation for the day:

Pre-activity check-in

Mark the strength of your feelings today on the scale below.

(1) (2) (3) (4) (5) (6) (7) (8) (9) (10)

(weak)   (strong)

What is my mood and the strength of this mood?

What are my main thoughts and the strength of these thoughts?

Post-activity check-in

Mark the strength of your feelings today on the scale below.

(1) (2) (3) (4) (5) (6) (7) (8) (9) (10)

(weak)   (strong)

What is my mood and the strength of this mood?

What are my main thoughts and the strength of these thoughts?

Reflections: How did this activity/today impact on me?

Learning: What did I learn about myself or my relationships today?

How will I apply this learning and/or take action?

What am I grateful for (internally or externally)?

Is there anything that I need to do in order to take care of myself today?

Did I use any positive coping strategies today?

☆ DAY 9 ☆ SELF-ACCEPTANCE

ACTIVITY OF THE DAY

Today's activity is based on the notion of 'radical acceptance', developed by Marsha Linehan. In essence, it means to fully accept our reality, including the challenging parts and emotions. When we fight these, they can gain more control over us. Acknowledging our life as it is and ourselves, as we are, can be empowering in the long term.

This activity is based around increasing self-acceptance. If you can, have a mirror available and do make sure that you are in a safe, undisturbed space. Spend at least twenty minutes on this activity.

1. First, think of one important event that has negatively impacted on your level of self-acceptance. Initially, do not choose an event that is too traumatic or overwhelming.

2. Now practise accepting this situation, with your mind and body. Use statements like 'I accept' or 'I forgive', if they feel right. It is key to note that you can accept or forgive people without needing to agree with their behaviour or invalidate your own feelings. Sometimes, letting go is a helpful thing to do for ourselves, on a practical and emotional level.

3. Notice any resistance in your body and sit with this until your body feels the emotions that it needs to.

Remind yourself that you cannot change what has happened, but the intensity of the emotion will decrease the more you lean into it. Remember that you have your grounding techniques available if you need them.

4. Bring yourself back to the present moment and, using a mirror if you wish, use a coping statement. There are some examples below – you could choose one that stands out to you, or more than one. Repeat the coping statement(s) out loud until you notice that you feel calmer and your body is more relaxed.

    -   I accept myself as I am

    -   I am safe in this moment

    -   I cannot change what has happened to me, but I can feel more empowered in this moment

    -   My past no longer controls me

    -   I love myself

    -   Although these feelings are uncomfortable, they will pass

    -   Life is still worth living, even when there is pain

    -   I have control over my present moment

    -   [A coping statement of your choice]

Take a breath and feel your feet on the floor.

DAILY REFLECTIVE JOURNAL

My chosen affirmation for the day:

Pre-activity check-in

Mark the strength of your feelings today on the scale below.

(1) (2) (3) (4) (5) (6) (7) (8) (9) (10)

(weak)   (strong)

What is my mood and the strength of this mood?

What are my main thoughts and the strength of these thoughts?

Post-activity check-in

Mark the strength of your feelings today on the scale below.

(1) (2) (3) (4) (5) (6) (7) (8) (9) (10)

(weak)   (strong)

What is my mood and the strength of this mood?

What are my main thoughts and the strength of these thoughts?

Reflections: How did this activity/today impact on me?

Learning: What did I learn about myself or my relationships today?

How will I apply this learning and/or take action?

What am I grateful for (internally or externally)?

Is there anything that I need to do in order to take care of myself today?

Did I use any positive coping strategies today?

☆ DAY 10 ☆ HAPPINESS

ACTIVITY OF THE DAY

Happiness is something we all strive to achieve, but we also all have our own version of what that is. Sometimes, we can equate happiness with what other people expect from or for us, or believe that achieving a certain goal, milestone or the acquisition of material possessions will lead to happiness. While all of these things can increase our happiness and satisfaction in the short term, it is also useful to work on our internal happiness so that we do not become dependent on external conditions to determine how happy we feel.

For today's activity, at the top of a piece of paper, write the words 'happiness is...' Then, to stop you from thinking too much, use your nondominant hand to write down anything that comes to mind. You can use words, full sentences, pictures, symbols or any other way of capturing what happiness means to you. You could record yourself talking if you don't want to write anything down. Don't overthink this; keep processing and recording until you come to a natural end.

Now use these reflections to write a paragraph outlining your version of happiness. Include what you could you do more of, any themes in what happiness means to you, what happiness feels like for you and any actions that you want to take to increase your level of internal happiness.

DAILY REFLECTIVE JOURNAL

My chosen affirmation for the day:

Pre-activity check-in

Mark the strength of your feelings today on the scale below.

(1) (2) (3) (4) (5) (6) (7) (8) (9) (10)

(weak)   (strong)

What is my mood and the strength of this mood?

What are my main thoughts and the strength of these thoughts?

Post-activity check-in

Mark the strength of your feelings today on the scale below.

(1) (2) (3) (4) (5) (6) (7) (8) (9) (10)

(weak)   (strong)

What is my mood and the strength of this mood?

What are my main thoughts and the strength of these thoughts?

Reflections: How did this activity/today impact on me?

Learning: What did I learn about myself or my relationships today?

How will I apply this learning and/or take action?

What am I grateful for (internally or externally)?

Is there anything that I need to do in order to take care of myself today?

Did I use any positive coping strategies today?

☆ DAY 11 ☆   FUTURE VISUALISATION

ACTIVITY OF THE DAY

How do you truly wish to live? Today's activity is a visualisation of your ideal future self. Take five minutes to complete this activity in a space where you will not be disturbed. Read through the script first – or you can access the audio version via my website. You can also record your own audio version and listen back to it.

If you can, and if it is safe to do so, close your eyes when you do this activity.

1. Feel your feet on the floor. Imagine that you are transported one year into the future and you are happy, healthy, content and generally fulfilled and coping well. What would you be doing? How would you be feeling? Which would be the key relationships in your life? What would you be thinking? Take a few moments to immerse yourself in this future self.

2. Now you are going to 'rewind' from your future self to your current self. Imagine that you are nine months ahead of your current life. What would you be doing? How would you be feeling? Which would be the key relationships in your life? What would you be thinking? What would you need to do to get yourself from your nine-month to your twelve-month future self? Write these actions down.

3. Imagine now that you are six months ahead of your current self. What would you be doing? How would you be feeling? Which would be the key relationships in your life? What would you be thinking? What would you need to do to get yourself from your six-month to your nine-month future self? Write these actions down.

4. Imagine that you are three months ahead of your current life. What would you be doing? How would you be feeling? Which would be the key relationships in your life? What would you be thinking? What would you need to do to get yourself from your three-month to your six-month future self? Write these actions down.

5. Now think about your current life. What are you doing? How are you feeling? Which are the key relationships in your life? What are you thinking? What would you need to do to get yourself from your current life to your three-month future self? Write down and commit to the actions that you will take in the next three months.

DAILY REFLECTIVE JOURNAL

My chosen affirmation for the day:

Pre-activity check-in

Mark the strength of your feelings today on the scale below.

(1) (2) (3) (4) (5) (6) (7) (8) (9) (10)
(weak)   (strong)

What is my mood and the strength of this mood?

What are my main thoughts and the strength of these thoughts?

Post-activity check-in

Mark the strength of your feelings today on the scale below.

(1) (2) (3) (4) (5) (6) (7) (8) (9) (10)
(weak)   (strong)

What is my mood and the strength of this mood?

What are my main thoughts and the strength of these thoughts?

Reflections: How did this activity/today impact on me?

Learning: What did I learn about myself or my relationships today?

How will I apply this learning and/or take action?

What am I grateful for (internally or externally)?

Is there anything that I need to do in order to take care of myself today?

Did I use any positive coping strategies today?

Chapter summary

This chapter has focused on helping us to go inward and to reflect on what is below the surface in terms of our authentic thoughts and feelings about ourselves. This can be an uncomfortable process, as we must face the truth of what we may have been avoiding. This reflecting gives us the opportunity to *choose* to think and feel differently about ourselves and to connect with the essence of who we are. Where we have been self-critical, we have the option of self-acceptance.

Self-acceptance forms the basis of our self-worth and self-love. It gives us the tools to begin to shape our narratives of ourselves and our inner world so that we can decide to take empowered action to do, think and be different. This is a dynamic, flowing, constant work in progress, so it can be useful to come back to the activities in this chapter to check in with yourself and your process. Self-acceptance gives you a chance to begin the healing and transformational journey from past pain and hurt to presence in the here and now. It allows you to retrain your attachment patterns to create relationship dynamics that feel safer and healthier. You are deserving of this investment in yourself.

In the next chapter, we will look at our external relationships to see how the outside world may be impacting our inside world.

3

My External World (Days 12–22)

The second section of this book, on your **external world**, is focused on your outer world and the key relationships around you. We are relational beings and we connect to others instinctually. Relationships help us to thrive and survive, whether this is family relationships, friendships or intimate partnerships. Often, we define who we are in the context of how we see ourselves and how we think we are perceived in these relationships; this in turn influences their dynamics.

In order to change our lives, we need to initially evaluate our key relationships. This may include asking questions such as, 'Are these relationships working for me?', 'Do they make me feel good?', 'Am I living the life that I deserve?', 'What needs to change?', 'How do I really feel about myself, in the now?' Rarely do we stop to reflect on these kinds of questions. Even when we do, are we inspired to take action to bring about change? Often we are not, unless a change has been forced by a crisis.

As discussed earlier in the book, our early attachments shape our relationship with ourselves; this then attracts other relationships that are aligned with our relational vibration. This is the cyclical nature of relationships. We tend to fall into the same patterns of relationships with others (and ourselves) based on the beliefs we have created about the role that we play in relationships, what we think we deserve and the conditions of worth that we have internalised (eg, 'I am worthy if I do X, Y, Z or if I behave in a certain way'). This is because patterns feel familiar, safe and predictable, whether or not they are in fact emotionally safe and healthy for us. They give us a benchmark of what to expect in life and from others. This section of the book will give you the tools to challenge some of these internalised beliefs and understand your attachment patterns.

Consider your inner circle

Think about the key people in your life, those you have the most contact with or you invest the most time or energy in. When you are engaged with or around them, how do you feel? How do you think? How do you behave? Below are a few questions to ask yourself about the core relationships in your life:

1. Do I feel valued in this relationship?

2. Do I feel emotionally and physically free in this relationship?

3. Am I able to express my true thoughts and feelings or do I feel judged?

4. How do I feel after being in contact with this person?

5. Is there trust and good communication in this relationship?

6. Do I feel accepted in this relationship for who I really am?

7. What characteristics does this person have in common with me and how do we differ from each other?

8. How do these characteristics align with who I am as a person and how I feel about life?

After you have answered these questions, review and re-evaluate your core relationships to see if there is anything that needs to be changed. Pay particular attention to relationships where you feel controlled, undervalued, undermined, criticised or emotionally unsafe, unable to be who you are. Ideally, your inner circle should contain people who empower and uplift you, particularly when you are vulnerable. This doesn't mean that they say what you want to hear all of the time, but they will tell you what you need to hear at that point in time, in a supportive manner, pushing you toward a better version of yourself.

You can say the same thing in many ways. Pay attention to how you feel when and after you interact with members of your inner circle. It is useful to pay attention to what I call the 'negative naysayers'. These are the people who have a problem for every solution and they can leave you drained, depleted, doubtful and feeling bad about yourself. These individuals often have a negative attitude toward [your] life and may be unsupportive of you reaching your true potential. Your interactions with them may also be one-sided, with the needs of the naysayer being the primary focus. As such, you may feel you are never able to communicate what you need, or the naysayer may devalue or compete with you. If you identify any naysayers in your life, ask yourself what the benefit of this relationship is to you (emotionally, mentally, physically and spiritually) and then consider if this is something you want or if it would benefit you to either shift positions or change the way that you interact with them. You cannot live a positive life when you are surrounded by negativity and you can't stand in your position of power if you have been drained of the energy you need to do so.

Boundaries

It is important to consciously set personal boundaries, which are the rules that regulate and contain our relationships. These signal what behaviour is OK with us and how we choose to be treated. We can choose to create healthier boundaries, for example by challenging ourselves to say no when we need to, or balancing the needs of others with our own needs. Healthy boundaries can help us to engage in emotional and physical intimacy in a way that feels safe for us, and allow us to express ourselves freely. We all have our own understanding of what boundaries mean to us. Some boundaries will be negotiable and others will not. Boundaries can be physical (touch and personal space), intellectual (thoughts, ideas, ideologies, life philosophies), emotional (based on how we process, acknowledge and express our emotions), sexual (including emotional and physical safety in sexual behaviour) and material (what material possessions, such as money, we are OK to share, in what amount and capacity and with whom). Boundaries are, again, linked to our self-image and internalised beliefs about ourselves and the world.

If we are trying to grow, evolve, adapt, learn or change, it is important to reflect on our inner circle. These are significant relationships that we can use as a barometer to how we feel, how we think, what we do, how we achieve, how we experience life and how we choose to define ourselves.

Co-dependency and rescuing patterns in relationships

It is important to acknowledge the role that we play in our relationships. One such role is of the **rescuer**. This is a person who wears the hero's cape and is always there for others, usually trying to help sort out their dramas, rescuing people in a practical or emotional sense. In a healthy relationship, there is mutuality in giving and receiving; a rescuer, though, is always giving more than they receive. This imbalance can lead to them feeling deflated, depleted, drained and lacking in energy. This is no wonder, when their energy, time and focus is always going to other people, meaning they have little left for themselves.

If being a rescuer is so draining, then why does the rescuer continue this pattern? There can be several reasons for this, but often it's because they want to feel needed. Usually, there is a positive impact on their self-esteem, self-worth or sense of purpose from rescuing one person after another and it can feel good. The rescuer may also have been conditioned into this role if it has been repeatedly validated. In this way, they can learn that they are worthy if they continue to rescue others. If someone consistently plays this role, others may *expect* it of them and they may seek out relationships that reinforce this pattern as it feels familiar to them.

It is unlikely that this desire to rescue others is coming from a negative or malicious place, and the rescuer may not even be aware of this unconscious drive or motivation but, even with the best will, this pattern does not help the other person in the relationship if they are put in a position where they are constantly being taken care of. In the long term, this can be disempowering for them as they do not learn how to self-manage or problem-solve. This can create emotional, psychological and/or physical **co-dependency**, which means to be overly reliant on someone. Rescuing and co-dependency often go hand in hand and there are people who like to be on the receiving end of a rescuing relationship. But the co-dependent person may struggle to realise their full potential, as they never learn to step into their own power, face challenges, build resilience or identify their own strengths.

The patterns in our relationships can become engrained, but we can also stop and reflect on whether they are healthy for ourselves and the other person or if things need to change. It is common in relationships for the individuals involved to become quite comfortable, on some level, in the predictability of the patterns that develop as they come to know, to a good extent, what to expect from the other person (their reactions, behaviours and/or responses). These emotional patterns and behaviours are usually replayed again and again and become the norm in that relationship, with both parties looping in with the other's patterns of behaviour, thought and emotion.

People often resist change as it can feel unpredictable and uncomfortable. We can get stuck in patterns that we gain something from (eg, feeling valued, being validated, physical connection). Alternatively, we can choose to change familiar patterns in relationships by reflecting on what is and isn't working in our lives and then taking small, consistent action steps toward change. It is also helpful to reflect on *why* you want to change the patterns in your relationships.

This chapter should give you more insight into the nature of your external relationships, what they mean to you and what changes you might want to make. It is important to note that you cannot force other people to change; you can only change the way that *you* feel, think and act. This is about focusing on changing things that you are aware of and are within your realm of control, such as your responses, mindset, boundaries, inner self-talk, beliefs, actions and where you focus your energy. We cannot control other people's beliefs, behaviours, opinions, judgements or actions. We also cannot change our past actions or completely control what happens in the future. But from my experience, if you begin to make consistent changes in your thoughts, in the way you regulate your emotions and your responses to people and situations, this will naturally have an impact on the relationships around you as you step out of your usual patterns of relating. Even though we are focusing on external relationships initially, the focus is on the 'you' within the 'us'.

☆ Day 12 ☆   SIMPLIFY YOUR LIFE

ACTIVITY OF THE DAY

As mentioned, there is a mind–body link. Our environment also plays a role in influencing these two things. For us to be able to organise our mental and emotional space, it is important to focus on our physical space, which can often be a representation of our inner mind. It may sound cliché, but ensuring that our physical space is as decluttered as possible helps with focus, mood and levels of motivation and achievement. Clearing out our physical 'stuff' can help us to start to clear out our emotional 'stuff'. It can also increase our energy over time, as we are less distracted by our environment.

This is as good a time as ever to challenge any tendency to procrastinate and feelings of being stuck. Procrastination is usually a form of avoidance, including seeking a distraction to avoid emotions. When decluttering in a conscious way, you can connect to any feelings that are coming up for you. This gives you an opportunity to identify and tackle any stressors, which can create a sense of achievement that boosts confidence and feelings of being in control.

Today, focus on the space around you. Which areas need decluttering or reorganising? You can choose to tackle as big or as small an area as you like, just get started today. If you don't want to declutter a physical space, you could do some digital decluttering, which can include things like social media accounts, how much time you spend on your devices, removing apps, clearing out old images and reorganising your phone.

Here are the steps to follow today:

1. **Step 1:** Identify your target clutter (which could be physical, mental/emotional, digital) and set yourself a time limit or specific task.

2. **Step 2:** Focus on what feelings come up for you as you engage in the decluttering process. Focus on your one task and try to remain in the moment.

3. **Step 3:** Review how you feel, including your thoughts and bodily sensations.

DAILY REFLECTIVE JOURNAL

My chosen affirmation for the day:

Pre-activity check-in

Mark the strength of your feelings today on the scale below.

(1) (2) (3) (4) (5) (6) (7) (8) (9) (10)

(weak)   (strong)

What is my mood and the strength of this mood?

What are my main thoughts and the strength of these thoughts?

Post-activity check-in

Mark the strength of your feelings today on the scale below.

(1) (2) (3) (4) (5) (6) (7) (8) (9) (10)

(weak)   (strong)

What is my mood and the strength of this mood?

What are my main thoughts and the strength of these thoughts?

Reflections: How did this activity/today impact on me?

Learning: What did I learn about myself or my relationships today?

How will I apply this learning and/or take action?

What am I grateful for (internally or externally)?

Is there anything that I need to do in order to take care of myself today?

Did I use any positive coping strategies today?

☆ Day 13 ☆ MINDFUL BEING

ACTIVITY OF THE DAY

Today's activity focuses on mindfulness techniques. Mindfulness, at its core, is about being present in the moment. Often, when we are anxious or stressed, we can be stuck either dwelling on the past or worrying about the future. Mindfulness can help us to become more focused on the here and now.

There are various techniques and lots of schools of thought on mindfulness. In essence, these are skills that can be developed – practice makes perfect. They can be good to use when your mind feels particularly full and can help with:

★ Clarity and focus, by increasing cognitive awareness and concentration

★ Improved physiological sensations

★ Better breathing

★ Encouraging self-compassion, kindness and acceptance

★ Feeling more relaxed

★ Supporting immunity

★ Staying present in the moment

There is a misconception that to practise mindfulness, you need to already be in a state of relaxed zen, have plenty of time to spare and be in a quiet space.

Today's technique can help you become more present in the now, whatever situation you're in, wherever you are. I see this as mindfulness that you can utilise on the go. It can help you become more attuned to your surroundings and more connected with yourself. Pick one of the following techniques to try today:

Colour and object spotting

Pick a colour, any colour. Wherever you are, notice anything in that colour or with that colour in it. As you do this, focus on both the big picture and smaller details in your surroundings. You could also pay attention to objects (big and small) around you. This will help you to feel more present, calmer and more relaxed.

New perspective

Another on-the-go mindfulness technique is to focus on an everyday item that is familiar to you, for example your phone, and pay close attention to it – notice the big and small details, the colours, the shape, the textures and see if you can observe anything new about it. This helps to focus your attention on one specific thing.

Five senses

In this activity, you identify five things that you can see, four things that you can hear, three things that you can touch, two things that you can smell and one thing that you can taste, engaging all five of your senses in everything that you are doing in the moment.

DAILY REFLECTIVE JOURNAL

My chosen affirmation for the day:

Pre-activity check-in

Mark the strength of your feelings today on the scale below.

(1) (2) (3) (4) (5) (6) (7) (8) (9) (10)
(weak)   (strong)

What is my mood and the strength of this mood?

What are my main thoughts and the strength of these thoughts?

Post-activity check-in

Mark the strength of your feelings today on the scale below.

(1) (2) (3) (4) (5) (6) (7) (8) (9) (10)
(weak)   (strong)

What is my mood and the strength of this mood?

What are my main thoughts and the strength of these thoughts?

Reflections: How did this activity/today impact on me?

Learning: What did I learn about myself or my relationships today?

How will I apply this learning and/or take action?

What am I grateful for (internally or externally)?

Is there anything that I need to do in order to take care of myself today?

Did I use any positive coping strategies today?

☆ Day 14 ☆ RADIATORS VERSUS DRAINS

ACTIVITY OF THE DAY

To function in our best capacity, there needs to be a balance in the energy that we are giving out (including the amount we are investing in others) versus the energy that we are receiving (including how much we feel invested in by others). When we feel good about this balance, it has a positive impact on our self-worth and self-esteem and ensures that our relationships are not one-sided or conditional. It is important to balance our emotional investments. We can think of this balancing act as like a see-saw. When one side is weighted heavier, we can feel drained or overwhelmed. When the balance is right, it can energise us.

There are people and things that 'heat us up', that inspire, energise and motivate us. These are our 'radiators'. Around them, we feel free to be ourselves without a fear of judgement or unrealistic expectations. We feel emotionally lighter, as we can clearly and authentically communicate and express our needs.

Then there are people and things that overwhelm, demotivate and deplete us. These are our 'drains'. When we are around them, we can feel emotionally or physically lacking in energy. We might even dread being around them or feel that they are demanding or have unrealistic expectations of us. In these relationships, it can feel that the power is weighted in their favour and we may be scared or unable to set healthy boundaries, such as being able to say no when needed.

Today's activity asks you identify your five key relationships and spend ten minutes identifying your radiators and drains. To do this, ask yourself: 'When I am interacting with this person, do I feel energised or drained?' Is the balance right or do you need to make some changes to how much you give or take? What could you do differently?

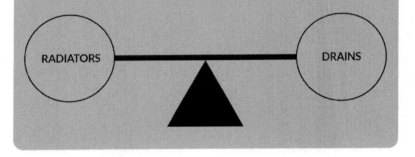

DAILY REFLECTIVE JOURNAL

My chosen affirmation for the day:

Pre-activity check-in

Mark the strength of your feelings today on the scale below.

(1) (2) (3) (4) (5) (6) (7) (8) (9) (10)
(weak)   (strong)

What is my mood and the strength of this mood?

What are my main thoughts and the strength of these thoughts?

Post-activity check-in

Mark the strength of your feelings today on the scale below.

(1) (2) (3) (4) (5) (6) (7) (8) (9) (10)
(weak)   (strong)

What is my mood and the strength of this mood?

What are my main thoughts and the strength of these thoughts?

Reflections: How did this activity/today impact on me?

Learning: What did I learn about myself or my relationships today?

How will I apply this learning and/or take action?

What am I grateful for (internally or externally)?

Is there anything that I need to do in order to take care of myself today?

Did I use any positive coping strategies today?

☆ Day 15 ☆   SELF-CARE CHECKLIST

ACTIVITY OF THE DAY

Self-care is not selfish; it's a form of self-love. Self-care is not a 'nice to have' add-on to life. It's essential to being able to function and deal with the people we encounter and the situations and external environment we find ourselves in. None of us can pour from an empty jug. In order to be able to be present and to give to others (if this is something we wish to do), we need to ensure that we first give to ourselves. This means taking care of our physical, mental and emotional health.

In that spirit, today you are going to spend ten minutes creating a self-care checklist for yourself. Below are some examples of self-care techniques that you can use as inspiration, or you may have your own:

Once you have identified some self-care strategies, the next step is to take action. How are you going to prioritise taking care of yourself? When will you engage in these activities? It's important to devise and stick to a self-care plan. Think of this as a skill that you're developing – the more you practise, the easier and more natural it will become. Use the following two statements to create your self-care plan.

Exercise	Dancing	Letting go
Eating well	Singing	Strength training
Limiting time on social media	Saying no	Making a plan of action
Regular breaks	Turning off your phone	Crystals
Finding a work–life balance	Talking to someone you trust about your feelings	Limiting your interactions with draining people
Positive thinking	Having a cup of tea	Practising gratitude
Breathing techniques	Going for a walk	Yoga
Having a bath	Lighting candles	Smiling
Getting enough sleep	Praying	Staying hydrated
Playing with pets	Writing or journaling	Resting
Crafting	Practising forgiveness	Cooking
Meditation	Getting organised	Mindfulness

My chosen self-care activities are:

My self-care plan is (eg, X activity for X amount of time):

DAILY REFLECTIVE JOURNAL

My chosen affirmation for the day:

Pre-activity check-in

Mark the strength of your feelings today on the scale below.

(1) (2) (3) (4) (5) (6) (7) (8) (9) (10)

(weak)   (strong)

What is my mood and the strength of this mood?

What are my main thoughts and the strength of these thoughts?

Post-activity check-in

Mark the strength of your feelings today on the scale below.

(1) (2) (3) (4) (5) (6) (7) (8) (9) (10)

(weak)   (strong)

What is my mood and the strength of this mood?

What are my main thoughts and the strength of these thoughts?

Reflections: How did this activity/today impact on me?

Learning: What did I learn about myself or my relationships today?

How will I apply this learning and/or take action?

What am I grateful for (internally or externally)?

Is there anything that I need to do in order to take care of myself today?

Did I use any positive coping strategies today?

☆ Day 16 ☆   MY TOP FIVE

ACTIVITY OF THE DAY

It is important to think about the people we spend the most time with, as they will have an impact on the way that we experience our world and ourselves within it. Today, take fifteen minutes to reflect on the top five people in your life. These are the people who you either spend the most time with or who consume more of your energy/thoughts.

For each individual, reflect on the following:

★ How do I feel when I am around/speak to this person, and afterwards?

★ How does this person impact on my thoughts? Are my thoughts usually more positive or negative after I interact with them?

★ What behaviours do I engage with afterwards and do they help me to manage my emotions (adaptive coping) or do I engage in behaviours that may not be ideal for my wellbeing?

Once you have reflected on these questions, consider if there are any changes or boundaries that need to be set or re-established.

DAILY REFLECTIVE JOURNAL

My chosen affirmation for the day:

Pre-activity check-in

Mark the strength of your feelings today on the scale below.

1   2   3   4   5   6   7   8   9   10
(weak)   (strong)

What is my mood and the strength of this mood?

What are my main thoughts and the strength of these thoughts?

Post-activity check-in

Mark the strength of your feelings today on the scale below.

1   2   3   4   5   6   7   8   9   10
(weak)   (strong)

What is my mood and the strength of this mood?

What are my main thoughts and the strength of these thoughts?

Reflections: How did this activity/today impact on me?

Learning: What did I learn about myself or my relationships today?

How will I apply this learning and/or take action?

What am I grateful for (internally or externally)?

Is there anything that I need to do in order to take care of myself today?

Did I use any positive coping strategies today?

☆ Day 17 ☆ MY SAFETY WHEEL

ACTIVITY OF THE DAY

To be able to fully engage in relationships, it's important that we feel safe. This can mean feeling physically and/or emotionally safe. Feeling safe means that we are able to overcome vulnerability to express our emotions and can honestly communicate how we feel and what we need, even if this means talking about difficult feelings. It also means we are able to tolerate differences (including in thoughts and opinions), without one party belittling the other or getting stuck in the rigidity of wanting to be 'right'. There is a flow in the relationship, rather than a conflict or power struggle. Both parties feel valued and respected. Safety is the foundation for a healthy relationship and gives us the opportunity to work through challenges, to grow and learn.

When thinking about close relationships, it can be useful to reflect on the following question:

Do I feel safe in this relationship (either emotionally or physically) to a point where I feel free to be my true self and communicate how I really feel?

Spend ten minutes using the safety wheel (see image below) to write down what you need in order to feel safe in a relationship, across the following categories:

★ Emotionally (eg, feeling relaxed, able to be your authentic self, unguarded and able to be emotionally vulnerable, feeling respected)

★ Physically (eg, feeling protected, absence of any threat of harm, good physical health)

★ Practically (eg, being in safe environments, being able to empathise, being kind and compassionate, being able to compromise, being able to respond to the needs of other key relationships, having healthy boundaries and communication, consistency in interactions)

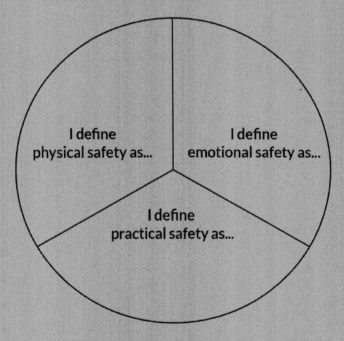

THE SAFETY WHEEL

Write down which of these elements are non-negotiable for you in a relationship in order for you to feel valued and able to express your authentic self.

Then pick one relationship to focus on for today. It could be a family member, a close friend or an intimate partner. Spend a few minutes thinking about the following questions:

★ How would you rate the level of safety in this relationship from 0–100 (with 0 as feeling unsafe and 100 as feeling completely safe at all levels)?

★ Are your non-negotiables being met?

★ What changes can you make to increase the feeling of safety for yourself?

DAILY REFLECTIVE JOURNAL

My chosen affirmation for the day:

Pre-activity check-in

Mark the strength of your feelings today on the scale below.

(1) (2) (3) (4) (5) (6) (7) (8) (9) (10)
(weak)   (strong)

What is my mood and the strength of this mood?

What are my main thoughts and the strength of these thoughts?

Post-activity check-in

Mark the strength of your feelings today on the scale below.

(1) (2) (3) (4) (5) (6) (7) (8) (9) (10)
(weak)   (strong)

What is my mood and the strength of this mood?

What are my main thoughts and the strength of these thoughts?

Reflections: How did this activity/today impact on me?

Learning: What did I learn about myself or my relationships today?

How will I apply this learning and/or take action?

What am I grateful for (internally or externally)?

Is there anything that I need to do in order to take care of myself today?

Did I use any positive coping strategies today?

☆ Day 18 ☆ LETTING GO OF CONTROL

ACTIVITY OF THE DAY

Today, you are going to reflect on the theme of control. Often, when we feel an intense emotion, such as frustration, anxiety or anger, it can be useful to reflect on why we may be feeling that way. At times, we can be trying to control things that are not within our control, such as a situation or other people's actions. This will inevitably lead to even more frustration and challenges. We cannot change or control other people. We can only change and control the way that we process, behave and respond to situations and people. This is not to say that emotions are 'good' or 'bad', just that we can always choose a different response.

Here are some examples of things you can control:

★ Your own thoughts

★ Your own behaviours

★ Practising self-care

★ Engaging in support

★ Measured risk-taking to move you toward a goal

Below are some things you can't control:

★ Other people's thoughts, feelings or behaviours

★ Other people's responses to you

★ Pleasing everyone

★ Future 'what ifs'

★ Another person's life

★ Every eventuality of how things may work out

Today, spend ten minutes reflecting on a challenging situation or relationship. Write down the answers to these questions:

★ What can I change?

★ What can't I change?

★ What can I let go of? (Eg, responsibility, guilt, shame, frustration, amount of contact etc.)

★ How can I take care of myself in this situation?

★ How will I decide to move forward in this situation?

DAILY REFLECTIVE JOURNAL

My chosen affirmation for the day:

Pre-activity check-in

Mark the strength of your feelings today on the scale below.

(1) (2) (3) (4) (5) (6) (7) (8) (9) (10)

(weak) (strong)

What is my mood and the strength of this mood?

What are my main thoughts and the strength of these thoughts?

Post-activity check-in

Mark the strength of your feelings today on the scale below.

(1) (2) (3) (4) (5) (6) (7) (8) (9) (10)

(weak) (strong)

What is my mood and the strength of this mood?

What are my main thoughts and the strength of these thoughts?

Reflections: How did this activity/today impact on me?

Learning: What did I learn about myself or my relationships today?

How will I apply this learning and/or take action?

What am I grateful for (internally or externally)?

Is there anything that I need to do in order to take care of myself today?

Did I use any positive coping strategies today?

☆ Day 19 ☆ PROBLEM-SOLVING CHECKLIST

ACTIVITY OF THE DAY

When we are dealing with a challenging person or situation, it can be easy to lose perspective and get stuck on what we perceive to be the problem. You can use the following checklist to work through any issues and move toward a solution-focused rather than a problem-focused approach.

Today, use this checklist to approach a (small or big) challenge that you're faced with. Spend ten minutes writing down your answers for steps one to five. Complete step six at the end of the day. Then, spend ten minutes on step seven.

Challenge checklist:

1. Describe the facts (not your feelings) about this situation.

2. Check the facts – are they definitely true?

3. Identify your goals – what do you want to be different in this scenario or what would you like to achieve? Why do you want to find a solution?

4. Think about potential solutions – it doesn't matter what they are, just get them down. What actions could you take? What support might you need?

5. Armed with this aeriel view, pick a solution that fits your goal.

6. Put the solution into action.

7. Evaluate the solution – did it work? Is there anything you could have done differently? What next steps could you take?

DAILY REFLECTIVE JOURNAL

My chosen affirmation for the day:

Pre-activity check-in

Mark the strength of your feelings today on the scale below.

(1) (2) (3) (4) (5) (6) (7) (8) (9) (10)

(weak)   (strong)

What is my mood and the strength of this mood?

What are my main thoughts and the strength of these thoughts?

Post-activity check-in

Mark the strength of your feelings today on the scale below.

(1) (2) (3) (4) (5) (6) (7) (8) (9) (10)

(weak)   (strong)

What is my mood and the strength of this mood?

What are my main thoughts and the strength of these thoughts?

Reflections: How did this activity/today impact on me?

Learning: What did I learn about myself or my relationships today?

How will I apply this learning and/or take action?

What am I grateful for (internally or externally)?

Is there anything that I need to do in order to take care of myself today?

Did I use any positive coping strategies today?

☆ Day 20 ☆ IDENTIFYING NEGATIVE THINKING PATTERNS

ACTIVITY OF THE DAY

Our thoughts are a powerful influence on how we feel and what we do. They shape the way we perceive ourselves, situations, other people, events and our world. We have tens of thousands of thoughts every day, so it is impossible to pay attention to every single one. Over time, our thoughts can become more automatic and familiar. It's like our brain gets to the point where it plays the same song again and again, but we can stop and reflect on whether we actually like that song or if we want to change the record.

Below, I have included some examples of negative thinking patterns, influenced by the cognitive behavioural therapy (CBT) model. A detailed description of CBT is beyond the scope of this book; however, as a starting point, readers are directed to the work of Beck, Greenberger and Padesky. In order to understand the current evidence for CBT, readers are directed to the NICE website.

As you read through these negative thinking patterns, highlight the errors that stand out to you or that you think that you may engage in.

★ Mind reading – assuming that we know what other people are thinking about us

★ Prediction – believing that we know what is going to happen in the future (usually something negative)

★ Critical self – putting ourselves down, blaming ourselves, not feeling like we are 'good enough'

★ 'Shoulds and musts' – putting pressure on ourselves to live up to unrealistic expectations (either our own or other people's)

★ Comparisons – seeing only the good in others and only the negative in ourselves

★ Mental filter – seeing the world in a negative way (with 'gloomy specs' on) and filtering out the positive

★ Black and white thinking – seeing things from a rigid, dual perspective and filtering out the grey eg, good/bad, right/wrong

★ Making judgements – judging people or situations based on our own perspective rather than the facts

★ Mountains and molehills – exaggerating negatives and minimising positives

★ Catastrophising – imagining, believing and expecting that the worst will happen

Today, you are simply going to observe your thoughts throughout the day to see if you can identify any negative thinking patterns. Note them down and see if you can spot any key themes, reoccurring negative thoughts or situations that make the thoughts worse.

Use this template:

1.   The negative thought patterns I noticed were...
2.   The key themes are...
3.   The situations that impacted on these thoughts were...

This can help to create more of an awareness and understanding of your negative thought patterns. We will return to this in tomorrow's activity.

DAILY REFLECTIVE JOURNAL

My chosen affirmation for the day:

Pre-activity check-in

Mark the strength of your feelings today on the scale below.

(1) (2) (3) (4) (5) (6) (7) (8) (9) (10)

(weak)   (strong)

What is my mood and the strength of this mood?

What are my main thoughts and the strength of these thoughts?

Post-activity check-in

Mark the strength of your feelings today on the scale below.

(1) (2) (3) (4) (5) (6) (7) (8) (9) (10)

(weak)   (strong)

What is my mood and the strength of this mood?

What are my main thoughts and the strength of these thoughts?

Reflections: How did this activity/today impact on me?

Learning: What did I learn about myself or my relationships today?

How will I apply this learning and/or take action?

What am I grateful for (internally or externally)?

Is there anything that I need to do in order to take care of myself today?

Did I use any positive coping strategies today?

☆ Day 21 ☆ THOUGHT CHALLENGING

ACTIVITY OF THE DAY

In the last activity, we focused on identifying negative thinking patterns; in this exercise, we are going to build on that to try to overcome them. Revisit yesterday's activity if you need to remind yourself of the types of unhelpful thinking patterns that are relevant to you.

The first step to reducing negative thoughts is to become more aware of them, which we began yesterday; the second step is to begin to consistently challenge them. Negative thinking patterns can make us believe that our negative thoughts are true, but it is important to check in with ourselves and with the facts. Are you seeing the situation for what it is or are you assuming the worst-case scenario? This exercise uses a CBT technique called thought challenging (Ellis, 2003).

Below is a table that you can use to challenge any negative thoughts that you may experience. This will help you, over time, to not presume these negative thoughts are true, but to get to a more balanced (and perhaps more positive) thought process and view of the world. As an example, I have filled in the thought challenging template below to show how you can use it. Spend at least ten minutes today proactively thought challenging.

THOUGHT CHALLENGING

Situation and physical reactions	Negative thoughts	Evidence for the thought	Evidence against the thought – what suggests that it might not be 100% true	Alternative thought
(Where did the negative thought occur?)	(You can also write down the type of thinking error if that is helpful)	(This means real evidence, not your sense of or feelings about it – evidence that would stand up in court)		(This can either be a more balanced or a more positive thought – but something which feels believable to you)
At work – about to give a presentation

Physical reaction: heart racing, sweaty palms, sweating | 'I am going to mess this up because I am awful at presentations.'

Type of thinking error: critical self | I messed up a presentation at uni three years ago. | I have done presentations since university and they have been OK.

There is no real evidence that I will fail in the here and now.

I have prepared and practised as much as I can. | This may feel scary, but being anxious about delivering a presentation is completely normal and I am as prepared as I can be.

I understand why I feel this way and I will simply try my best. |

BLANK THOUGHT CHALLENGING TEMPLATE:

Situation and physical reactions (Where did the negative thought occur?)	Negative thoughts (You can also write down the type of thinking error if that is helpful)	Evidence for the thought (This means real evidence, not your sense of or feelings about it – evidence that would stand up in court)	Evidence against the thought – what suggests that it might not be 100% true	Alternative thought (This can either be a more balanced or a more positive thought – but something which feels believable to you)
Situation: Physical reaction:	Negative thought: Type of thinking error:	Factual evidence for the thought:	Factual evidence against the thought:	Alternative, more balanced thought:

DAILY REFLECTIVE JOURNAL

My chosen affirmation for the day:

Pre-activity check-in

Mark the strength of your feelings today on the scale below.

(1) (2) (3) (4) (5) (6) (7) (8) (9) (10)
(weak)   (strong)

What is my mood and the strength of this mood?

What are my main thoughts and the strength of these thoughts?

Post-activity check-in

Mark the strength of your feelings today on the scale below.

(1) (2) (3) (4) (5) (6) (7) (8) (9) (10)
(weak)   (strong)

What is my mood and the strength of this mood?

What are my main thoughts and the strength of these thoughts?

Reflections: How did this activity/today impact on me?

Learning: What did I learn about myself or my relationships today?

How will I apply this learning and/or take action?

What am I grateful for (internally or externally)?

Is there anything that I need to do in order to take care of myself today?

Did I use any positive coping strategies today?

☆ Day 22 ☆   'I AM' STATEMENTS

As we have seen from the previous exercises, the way that we speak to ourselves is of crucial importance and can skew our perception of ourselves. Our self-perception can also be influenced by our key relationships and the people around us. Sometimes, we internalise these perceptions without realising and this can shape how we live.

Grounding/power statements and positive affirmations can be used to bring your awareness back to the here and now. They are particularly helpful if you are having anxious or negative thoughts, as a way to challenge this thinking. Depending on the context, what you are feeling anxious about or what your negative thoughts are related to, you can use an 'I am' statement to challenge these thoughts. For example, if I was having anxious thoughts about feeling unsafe, with no real evidence that my safety is truly at risk, I may choose 'I am safe' as a grounding statement. If I was having negative thoughts related to a lack of self-confidence, I might choose a statement like 'I am good enough', 'I am worthy', 'I am improving daily' or 'I am a work in progress'.

ACTIVITY OF THE DAY

Today's exercise focuses on helping you to affirm a new perception of yourself by creating 'I am' power statements. The words 'I am' are hugely powerful and they set the tone for how you see yourself, how you interact with others and what you feel you are deserving of. Thoughts won't change overnight, but making an effort to consciously affirm your power statements will help to change your thoughts, feelings and behaviours over time. There are two steps to this process, outlined below:

1. **Write a positives list.** This is a list of all of the internal attributes that you have and that no one can take away from you; it is what makes you who you are and it is usually connected to your values. You do not have to come up with masses of things, particularly if this feels difficult at first. You may also wish to reflect on what people who know you might say about you – eg, kind, caring, fun, loyal, diligent, creative, passionate, resilient, confident and so on. Spend at least ten minutes doing this and try to come up with at least ten items to begin with (you can keep adding to your list as you recognise more attributes through the evidence that you gather from your interactions). Highlight or indicate in some way 2–5 of the positive attributes on this list that stand out; we will use these items in the next step.

2. **Create your 'I am' statement.** Ideally, this should be taken from your positives list. What parts of yourself would you like to consciously focus on and solidify, or what would you like to feel more of? You can come up with as many statements as you like. Here are some examples:

   - I am confident
   - I am happy
   - I am secure
   - I am mindful
   - I am balanced

Make one of these 'I am' statements your daily affirmation. Then commit to affirming this daily for a set period of time, perhaps 30 days.

You can affirm the statement in several ways, including:

★ Repeating the statement out loud.

★ Recording yourself saying the statement and listening back.

★ Saying it to yourself in the mirror.

★ Writing it down.

★ Having reminders of it on post-it notes, a vision board or as a screenshot on your phone.

★ Using butterfly tapping to embody the statement. In this method, you close your eyes and cross your arms, as if you're giving yourself a hug. You then start tapping on your upper arms, alternating your right and left hands. Get into a rhythm with your tapping and remember to keep alternating right then left. As you tap, you say the 'I am' statement either in your head or out loud, until you start to notice a shift in how you feel, either in your body or emotionally.

Some people like to create a series of affirmations and/or grounding statements that they say to themselves a few times a day, or keep to hand somewhere where they can see them, so that they can regularly challenge negative thinking patterns. Remember, this is a process that takes consistency and practice. I have also included some affirmation cards and a template for creating your own toward the end of this book.

DAILY REFLECTIVE JOURNAL

My chosen affirmation for the day:

Pre-activity check-in

Mark the strength of your feelings today on the scale below.

(1) (2) (3) (4) (5) (6) (7) (8) (9) (10)
(weak)   (strong)

What is my mood and the strength of this mood?

What are my main thoughts and the strength of these thoughts?

Post-activity check-in

Mark the strength of your feelings today on the scale below.

(1) (2) (3) (4) (5) (6) (7) (8) (9) (10)
(weak)   (strong)

What is my mood and the strength of this mood?

What are my main thoughts and the strength of these thoughts?

Reflections: How did this activity/today impact on me?

Learning: What did I learn about myself or my relationships today?

How will I apply this learning and/or take action?

What am I grateful for (internally or externally)?

Is there anything that I need to do in order to take care of myself today?

Did I use any positive coping strategies today?

Chapter summary

This chapter has begun to highlight the important link between what we feel, what we think and what we do. The practices of bringing ourselves back to the present help with creating objectivity in the now, so that we can ensure we are living in the moment rather than being influenced by the events of the past or our worries about the future. With more objectivity, we learn to *respond* rather than *react*, which helps to improve our decision making and problem-solving skills.

It can also be an empowering process as, rather than *feeling* that we have no control, we can start to focus on the things that we can control. In this way, we realise that the power for making long-lasting changes lives within us.

This chapter provides the fundamental snapshot of your life in the now that you need in order to see what is working for you and where you can make changes or set boundaries, for yourself or others. The light bulb of awareness is now on, but we cannot ignore what came before this moment. In order to better under-stand ourselves and our self-perception, we need to understand the influence of the combination of our internal and external experiences. The next section will address this further. Are you ready to step into your authenticity?

4

My True Self (Days 23–30)

The third section, on your **true self**, helps you to link in with who you really are in this moment and your needs, wants and desires. It will help you to blend the learnings from the first two sections, with the aim of helping you to live a more authentic life in the now.

It is rare that we show people who we truly are. Typically, we are conditioned into presenting a flawless version of ourselves based on what we feel we 'should' be. We often acquire these 'shoulds' from our early attachments, through family and societal norms and other people's expectations of us. This can lead to us limiting who we are and what we show the world or people we have relationships with; we can hide behind this idealised mask, as it feels safer to us and less exposing. It can also lead us to have unrealistic expectations of ourselves and others, for example, expecting perfection or seeing ourselves as having failed if we do not meet our idealised standards. This is all or nothing thinking, which is too rigid. We can continue to do this for several years to a point where this way of relating to the world feels normal and automatic, a part of our subconscious behaviour.

But the more we hide behind a mask, the greater the possibility that we become detached from our true selves, the authentic essence of who we are. It is useful to take time to reflect on who we really are in order to try and bring subconscious patterns of relating, feelings, thoughts and behaviours into the conscious mind. It can help us to shine a light on some of the 'shoulds' that we are living our life by to consider whether we are living a life full of growth or full of limitation. It is challenging to live by other people's rules and it can impact how we feel about ourselves. It is impossible to please everybody. Getting more in touch with our true selves helps us to nurture ourselves in a kind, loving and compassionate way – to turn down the volume on the voice of the inner critic in our head holding us back (even if from a desire to 'protect' us from fear or vulnerability). When we have a better awareness of who we are, we can begin to reflect on what is working in our lives, what truly matters to us and what needs to change. We can then choose to take empowered actions toward a more authentic life.

You can also choose not to take action – that's OK too. The key thing is that as your awareness increases, you will get into the flow of making more informed decisions based on who you are and how you want to live your life. It helps you to understand the patterns of how you relate to yourself and others, making this less automatic. It gives you the tools to consciously flow with any changes in yourself or your life. It also gives you the opportunity to let go of or change the things that no longer serve you or make you feel good. Knowing and accepting yourself for who you are in the now is the secret to true empowerment.

☆ Day 23 ☆   EMOTIONAL CHECK-IN

ACTIVITY OF THE DAY

Today's activity is about how you can create more of a balance in your life as you pause for moments of reflection. Building in reflective time means that we are providing space for any anxieties, so that we can validate our feelings and needs. It also provides an opportunity to proactively address self-care. This can help to shift us out of a more reactive mode into a more reflective mode.

Step 1: Take ten minutes today to write a paragraph for each of the following reflections:

★ The dominant emotion I am feeling right now is...

★ My current thoughts are...

★ Right now, my physical body feels...

★ What I need in this moment is...

Step 2: Take some action based on the reflections.

As a note, I encourage people to regularly check in on their emotions. This can be done through journaling, using the questions in this activity as regular prompts. This will help you to pre-empt challenges as well as identify possible strategies to overcome them. Over time, this will shift you from a more problem-focused to a more solution-focused way of being.

DAILY REFLECTIVE JOURNAL

My chosen affirmation for the day:

Pre-activity check-in

Mark the strength of your feelings today on the scale below.

(1) (2) (3) (4) (5) (6) (7) (8) (9) (10)
(weak)   (strong)

What is my mood and the strength of this mood?

What are my main thoughts and the strength of these thoughts?

Post-activity check-in

Mark the strength of your feelings today on the scale below.

(1) (2) (3) (4) (5) (6) (7) (8) (9) (10)
(weak)   (strong)

What is my mood and the strength of this mood?

What are my main thoughts and the strength of these thoughts?

Reflections: How did this activity/today impact on me?

Learning: What did I learn about myself or my relationships today?

How will I apply this learning and/or take action?

What am I grateful for (internally or externally)?

Is there anything that I need to do in order to take care of myself today?

Did I use any positive coping strategies today?

☆ Day 24 ☆ ENHANCING SELF-LOVE

ACTIVITY OF THE DAY

Self-love is a term that we hear often but, like self-care, it is a highly individual construct. When we show ourselves love, we are in a state of accepting and appreciating our uniqueness. This means that we can accept our perceived flaws or inadequacies in a kind and compassionate way, leaving the space to invest in ourselves so that we can grow and change. Over time, greater self-love helps us to feel more grounded and to build resilience. We become more confident and comfortable in knowing who we are.

Self-love isn't about seeing or seeking perfection. It is the knowledge that we can be 'good enough' and a work in progress at the same time. Self-love helps us to challenge self-criticism. When we love ourselves, we act in a way that shows that we value ourselves. We develop a relationship with ourselves where we take care of our emotional, physical, spiritual and mental needs so that we can take risks to improve and enhance our wellbeing. Self-love is a continuous journey and involves reflecting on how we balance our own needs with the needs of others.

For today's activity, spend ten minutes answering the following questions:

★ What does self-love mean to me?

★ If I was showing myself healthy levels of self-love, how would I be feeling or what would I be doing?

- Physically (eg, nutrition, exercise, sleep, enjoyable activities)?

- Emotionally (eg, calm, relaxed, confident, content)?

- Mentally (eg, positive thinking patterns, praising self)?

Having reflected on the above, now focus on the following questions linked to action:

★ What is one small action step that I can take today to show myself more self-love?

★ What longer-term action(s) can I take to incorporate more self-love into my life and what support might I need to help me do this?

DAILY REFLECTIVE JOURNAL

My chosen affirmation for the day:

Pre-activity check-in

Mark the strength of your feelings today on the scale below.

(1) (2) (3) (4) (5) (6) (7) (8) (9) (10)

(weak)   (strong)

What is my mood and the strength of this mood?

What are my main thoughts and the strength of these thoughts?

Post-activity check-in

Mark the strength of your feelings today on the scale below.

(1) (2) (3) (4) (5) (6) (7) (8) (9) (10)

(weak)   (strong)

What is my mood and the strength of this mood?

What are my main thoughts and the strength of these thoughts?

Reflections: How did this activity/today impact on me?

Learning: What did I learn about myself or my relationships today?

How will I apply this learning and/or take action?

What am I grateful for (internally or externally)?

Is there anything that I need to do in order to take care of myself today?

Did I use any positive coping strategies today?

☆ Day 25 ☆ FINDING MY CORE VALUES

ACTIVITY OF THE DAY

Today you will focus on identifying your core values. Our core values are those that we deem to be most important. They provide the framework for our sense of self and influence how we live our lives. When we are living in alignment with our core values, this positively impacts our level of motivation, our sense of accomplishment and how happy and satisfied we feel. It can create a sense that we are 'living with purpose'.

Our core values are also present in and influence our relationships with others and how we see ourselves in relation to other people. It is important to re-evaluate our core values to ensure they are true to our genuine selves and not values that may have been imposed on us or that we have been conditioned to uphold. Here are some examples of a few possible core values to help stimulate your thinking:

Respect	Open-mindedness	Dependability
Curiosity	Passion	Honesty
Attentiveness	Kindness	Freedom
Compassion	Friendliness	Warmth
Motivation	Confidence	Humility
Consistency	Ambition	Contentment
Ethical living	Sensitivity	Responsibility
Transparency	Trust	Achievement
Stability (emotional, financial etc)	Connection	Integrity
Self-growth	Communication	Positive outlook
Creativity	Happiness	Joy
Self-expression	Balance	Self-care
Adventure	Usefulness	

Spend ten minutes, without judgement or trying to control the process, noting down all of the values that are important to you.

Out of this list, highlight your top ten. These are your most important, non-negotiable values. Are these values represented in your key relationships? If not, how can this be changed? For example, by setting healthier boundaries, asking for what you need, limiting interactions. Write down three ideas for how you can better align your key relationships with your core values.

This activity is about giving you space to re-evaluate what values you are holding onto to see if they are aligned to what is important to you as you work toward creating a life that feels more authentic to you.

DAILY REFLECTIVE JOURNAL

My chosen affirmation for the day:

Pre-activity check-in

Mark the strength of your feelings today on the scale below.

(1) (2) (3) (4) (5) (6) (7) (8) (9) (10)

(weak)   (strong)

What is my mood and the strength of this mood?

What are my main thoughts and the strength of these thoughts?

Post-activity check-in

Mark the strength of your feelings today on the scale below.

(1) (2) (3) (4) (5) (6) (7) (8) (9) (10)

(weak)   (strong)

What is my mood and the strength of this mood?

What are my main thoughts and the strength of these thoughts?

Reflections: How did this activity/today impact on me?

Learning: What did I learn about myself or my relationships today?

How will I apply this learning and/or take action?

What am I grateful for (internally or externally)?

Is there anything that I need to do in order to take care of myself today?

Did I use any positive coping strategies today?

☆ Day 26 ☆ SPEAKING MY TRUTH

ACTIVITY OF THE DAY

This activity is a useful way to continue to build on being less reactive and more responsive in your interactions. The FAAB model, outlined below, can help you to balance speaking your authentic truth with staying grounded and logical. In this way, you can express your emotions, thoughts and feelings without getting caught up in them. The model can be applied to a range of scenarios and situations, from work environments to personal relationships.

Facts: This is the point where you simply state the facts of the situation, rather than expressing your feelings.

Acknowledge: This is where you acknowledge your feelings and begin to take responsibility for your feelings, by using 'I' statements.

Assert: You can assert yourself by asking for what you want or setting healthier boundaries, which may include saying no.

Balance: This is about negotiating and balance. What advantage does the other person in the interaction gain from cooperating with you? For example: 'If we cooperate, then...' 'We are both invested in trying to resolve this', 'Working together will be beneficial for us both', 'It's important for me to find a balance in my life, as I am sure it is for you' etc.

Use the FAAB model in one of your interactions today.

DAILY REFLECTIVE JOURNAL

My chosen affirmation for the day:

Pre-activity check-in

Mark the strength of your feelings today on the scale below.

(1) (2) (3) (4) (5) (6) (7) (8) (9) (10)
(weak)   (strong)

What is my mood and the strength of this mood?

What are my main thoughts and the strength of these thoughts?

Post-activity check-in

Mark the strength of your feelings today on the scale below.

(1) (2) (3) (4) (5) (6) (7) (8) (9) (10)
(weak)   (strong)

What is my mood and the strength of this mood?

What are my main thoughts and the strength of these thoughts?

Reflections: How did this activity/today impact on me?

Learning: What did I learn about myself or my relationships today?

How will I apply this learning and/or take action?

What am I grateful for (internally or externally)?

Is there anything that I need to do in order to take care of myself today?

Did I use any positive coping strategies today?

☆ Day 27 ☆ COPING SAFETY NET

ACTIVITY OF THE DAY

This technique is a great way to help you develop the resources that you need to deal with life overall. We are often more resilient than we give ourselves credit for. Particularly when we are under stress, feel overwhelmed or are facing a challenge, it can be easier to focus on the negatives and harder to remember our internal strengths. These strengths are our internal resources. These resources are things that can help us to cope with our current situation, that we can always tap into, even if external circumstances and other people's behaviour are outside of our control.

Today, spend ten minutes thinking about a recent challenge that you overcame.

★ What was the challenge?

★ What did you do? (Eg, problem-solved, sought out information, voiced your needs, moved your body, talked to others, took a break.)

★ What does this say about you? (Eg, resourceful, resilient, empowered, creative, able to express yourself, reliable.)

Now turn these into 'I am' statements and repeat these out loud for two minutes. It can be useful to reflect on your strengths during challenging times, as this helps to reinforce that you are capable and able to overcome challenges, both in the here and now and in the future.

DAILY REFLECTIVE JOURNAL

My chosen affirmation for the day:

Pre-activity check-in

Mark the strength of your feelings today on the scale below.

(1) (2) (3) (4) (5) (6) (7) (8) (9) (10)

(weak)   (strong)

What is my mood and the strength of this mood?

What are my main thoughts and the strength of these thoughts?

Post-activity check-in

Mark the strength of your feelings today on the scale below.

(1) (2) (3) (4) (5) (6) (7) (8) (9) (10)

(weak)   (strong)

What is my mood and the strength of this mood?

What are my main thoughts and the strength of these thoughts?

Reflections: How did this activity/today impact on me?

Learning: What did I learn about myself or my relationships today?

How will I apply this learning and/or take action?

What am I grateful for (internally or externally)?

Is there anything that I need to do in order to take care of myself today?

Did I use any positive coping strategies today?

☆ Day 28 ☆ — SYMBOL OF EMPOWERMENT

ACTIVITY OF THE DAY

This activity is about finding a way to empower yourself in challenging situations. You will need an A4 piece of paper and a pen. It would also be useful to find a space where you will not be disturbed for ten to fifteen minutes.

Start by reflecting on two questions:

★ What is the situation that is troubling you?

★ What emotional resource do you need in order to feel more empowered? Eg, confidence, calmness, expression etc. Think of one word, ideally.

At the top of your piece of paper, write the word that you have identified. If there was a symbol that represented this word, what would it be? Don't overthink this, just see what comes to mind straight away, even if the connection doesn't seem logical or obvious.

For the next stage, using your nondominant hand draw the symbol that came to mind in the middle of the piece of paper, as big or as small as you like. Don't spend too long drawing or perfecting this, this isn't about artistic skill – any way that the symbol comes out is OK. The reason for using your nondominant hand is that it activates both hemispheres of your brain and opens the possibility of more creativity and less control, as you bypass your adult logic and access your inner child. This can help to reduce levels of stress and anxiety (Annett, 1985; Philip and Frey, 2016).

Now come to a standing position and put your piece of paper on the floor. Notice how your body feels now and what your posture is like. Now stand on your power symbol (preferably with your eyes closed) and imagine what you would feel like if you truly embodied the word. For example, if your resource is confidence, how would you feel if you were confident? Notice your posture, emotions and bodily sensations. Tap this new feeling in for a few minutes, either through butterfly tapping or tapping on your knees (see the Additional Resources section for instructions on how to do this).

You can step back into this stance at any time by changing your posture and physical sensations so that they are more aligned with the empowered and resourced you.

You may wish to go through the process again and create either a series of symbols (so that you can pick which one you need) or a symbol that is relevant to another situation where you would like to feel more emotionally grounded and in control of your reactions.

DAILY REFLECTIVE JOURNAL

My chosen affirmation for the day:

Pre-activity check-in

Mark the strength of your feelings today on the scale below.

(1) (2) (3) (4) (5) (6) (7) (8) (9) (10)
(weak)   (strong)

What is my mood and the strength of this mood?

What are my main thoughts and the strength of these thoughts?

Post-activity check-in

Mark the strength of your feelings today on the scale below.

(1) (2) (3) (4) (5) (6) (7) (8) (9) (10)
(weak)   (strong)

What is my mood and the strength of this mood?

What are my main thoughts and the strength of these thoughts?

Reflections: How did this activity/today impact on me?

Learning: What did I learn about myself or my relationships today?

How will I apply this learning and/or take action?

What am I grateful for (internally or externally)?

Is there anything that I need to do in order to take care of myself today?

Did I use any positive coping strategies today?

☆ Day 29 ☆ MY CHAMPION'S STORY

ACTIVITY OF THE DAY

As highlighted throughout this book, you may encounter several internalised barriers that could impact you reaching your full potential and your ability to live your most authentic life. This book has helped you start the process of identifying and challenging some of these barriers, including fear, blocks to confidence, self-love, self-belief and feelings of worthiness.

Today's activity is about recognising the essence of who you are – a champion. A champion is someone who may have faced several challenges and setbacks on their journey, but has still accomplished great things and is victorious in many ways. They are a warrior, not a worrier. They use their mental agility and strength to overcome adversity – this is what we've been working on building throughout this book.

Today, you are going to write your own champion's story. Write from an 'I am' perspective. You can reflect on the prompts below and include them in your champion's story, which should be about two or three paragraphs long.

★ What makes you who you are? What is your uniqueness?

★ What is important to you in life? What do you care about?

★ How have you overcome challenges and what does this say about you and your abilities?

★ What is it that you want from life and how will you commit to moving toward this?

This process is about seeing the greatness that is inside you, what you have to offer the world and relationships. It can then be used as a reminder of your power. What direction will you choose to take your champion's story in?

DAILY REFLECTIVE JOURNAL

My chosen affirmation for the day:

Pre-activity check-in

Mark the strength of your feelings today on the scale below.

(1) (2) (3) (4) (5) (6) (7) (8) (9) (10)
(weak)   (strong)

What is my mood and the strength of this mood?

What are my main thoughts and the strength of these thoughts?

Post-activity check-in

Mark the strength of your feelings today on the scale below.

(1) (2) (3) (4) (5) (6) (7) (8) (9) (10)
(weak)   (strong)

What is my mood and the strength of this mood?

What are my main thoughts and the strength of these thoughts?

Reflections: How did this activity/today impact on me?

Learning: What did I learn about myself or my relationships today?

How will I apply this learning and/or take action?

What am I grateful for (internally or externally)?

Is there anything that I need to do in order to take care of myself today?

Did I use any positive coping strategies today?

☆ Day 30 ☆ VISION BOARD

ACTIVITY OF THE DAY

This last exercise is about creating a future vision for your life. As I'm sure you can see by now, self-development and change is an ongoing process and it is useful to stop and review your progress.

You may have heard of a vision board or even created one yourself previously. They are a great way to re-evaluate your goals and priorities and stay focused on what you want to achieve and how you want to feel, to reflect and stay motivated. You can be as creative as you like; you can use words, drawings, symbols, magazine cut outs, stickers, colours or any other method of your choosing to create your vision board. Keep it (or a picture of it) in a place where you will see it regularly. You could also create one online using an app, or make a picture album on your phone.

Here are some areas that you may choose to focus on:

★ Personal growth
★ Relationships (friendships, romantic relationships, relationship with yourself)
★ Self-love
★ Physical health
★ Home
★ Family
★ Career

- ★ Leisure/fun
- ★ Emotional health
- ★ Travel
- ★ Hobbies/skill development
- ★ Money/income
- ★ Spirituality/faith

You might choose one area or several, depending on what feels important to you and what aligns to your goals, priorities and values. For each of the areas, identify what it is you want to achieve, how you would like to feel and what action steps you can take to get you there. You may want to break these goals into smaller goals and review them regularly to see if there has been a shift, for example at three months, six months, nine months or one year.

Spend at least twenty minutes on today's exercise.

DAILY REFLECTIVE JOURNAL

My chosen affirmation for the day:

Pre-activity check-in

Mark the strength of your feelings today on the scale below.

(1) (2) (3) (4) (5) (6) (7) (8) (9) (10)
(weak)   (strong)

What is my mood and the strength of this mood?

What are my main thoughts and the strength of these thoughts?

Post-activity check-in

Mark the strength of your feelings today on the scale below.

(1) (2) (3) (4) (5) (6) (7) (8) (9) (10)
(weak)   (strong)

What is my mood and the strength of this mood?

What are my main thoughts and the strength of these thoughts?

Reflections: How did this activity/today impact on me?

Learning: What did I learn about myself or my relationships today?

How will I apply this learning and/or take action?

What am I grateful for (internally or externally)?

Is there anything that I need to do in order to take care of myself today?

Did I use any positive coping strategies today?

Chapter summary

The aim of this chapter was to bypass the noise of expectations, whether your own or those of other people, to help you reconnect with your inner goals, values, wants, needs, self-image and desires. If you wish to make long-lasting changes, you will need to continually commit to this process. Reflecting on your internal and external worlds in this way will help you to ascertain how aligned you are to an authentic way of living, so that you can reflect on what actions you can take to get things back on track.

To stay on track, make a pledge to yourself. This is a way of ensuring that you do not get lost in the inner and outer chatter, disconnecting you from yourself. It should be based around a personal core values statement, identifying your top five core values that are authentic to you and will influence the way you choose to live your life and interact with others moving forward. These are your non-negotiables and can be utilised to check in with yourself and how content and satisfied you feel in your life. I have included an example pledge, but do make this your own.

My pledge

I, ... [your name here],
recognise that I am worthy and that I deserve to invest
in myself as a way to aid my healthy connection to
others and to live a fulfilling and satisfying life.

To achieve this, I choose to live my life in accordance
with the following non-negotiable values: ....
.... [write your values here]

The reason why it's important for me to use these
guiding principles to live an authentic life in this way is:
....
....
.... [state your reason
here – this 'why' will remind you of the importance of
this process at times when you feel less motivated]

The signs that I am not living my life in accordance with
these values are: ....
....
.... [changes in feelings, thoughts,
behaviours, motivation etc]

If I notice any of these signs, I will: ....
....
.... [list some positive
coping strategies and sources of support]

5
What Next?

Like the initial commitment you made to yourself, it can be useful to forge an ongoing, reviewable commitment and a set of goals to help you to stay on track. It can be hard to recognise just how far we have come. This is why you were asked to set initial personal goals and to rate yourself using the quick check-in tool at the beginning of the book. Rate yourself again below and then look at your answers from your first check-in to notice any changes, patterns or trends. This can also help to identify the areas of your life where you could benefit from extra support or where you may need to be kinder to yourself. Reviewing things in this way will support you in the development of your longer-term personal goals. This is not about perfection; it's about reflection.

Identifying any gaps between where you currently are and where you want to be can create opportunities to assert yourself and better meet your needs, understand your emotions, access support or make empowered changes that align more authentically with the real you. Hopefully, you will have discovered that there is a benefit in sitting with and consciously exploring your thoughts and feelings in order to try and understand them and yourself better. This gives your mind back its power.

After 30 days: Check-in and personal goals

Rate yourself on the following statements (where 1 is low and 10 is high):

I am happy.

(1) (2) (3) (4) (5) (6) (7) (8) (9) (10)
(weak)   (strong)

I am confident.

(1) (2) (3) (4) (5) (6) (7) (8) (9) (10)
(weak)   (strong)

I am of value.

(1) (2) (3) (4) (5) (6) (7) (8) (9) (10)
(weak)   (strong)

I am content.

(1) (2) (3) (4) (5) (6) (7) (8) (9) (10)
(weak)   (strong)

My life is balanced.

(1) (2) (3) (4) (5) (6) (7) (8) (9) (10)
(weak)   (strong)

I listen to my needs.

(1) (2) (3) (4) (5) (6) (7) (8) (9) (10)
(weak)   (strong)

I am able to say no when I need to.

(weak)   (strong)

I feel secure in my life.

(weak)   (strong)

My vinyl wheel

Again, use the vinyl wheel template to plot out how satisfied you are with each of the following areas of your life (with 10 being 'very satisfied' and 0 being 'not satisfied'). You can use a coloured pencil to mark where you think you are in each of the following areas:

Below are some prompts for you to reflect on:

★   What changes have I made?

★   What other changes would I like to make?

★   I will continue to take good care of myself by...

★   The personal goals I want to continue to work on, which are aligned with my personal values, are...

★   I am motivated to make these changes because... (Come back to this 'why' when you need to)

★   I will work toward achieving these goals by taking these action steps...

★   I have developed these positive coping strategies to help me to manage my feelings, thoughts and behaviours...

★   The protective/positive things/people in my life are...

★   My internal strengths are...

Chapter summary

It is important to regularly review our state of being. A key take-away is the link between feelings, thoughts and actions. While it is great to focus on behaviour, you will have realised that also paying attention to your emotions and thoughts is an essential part of shifting your mindset and making long-lasting changes and habits. It is the basis of unlearning what no longer serves you so that you can strengthen your relationship with yourself. With persistence and consistency over time, this will naturally enhance your self-image and the quality of all your relationships.

The magic to make empowered changes lies within you.

Conclusion

I hope that this book has highlighted that we are all on our own journey, influenced by both our external and internal worlds. The process of navigating this journey is not always easy. It takes courage to curiously explore who we are and let go of the conditions that have been placed upon us. Self-awareness can be challenging. But even if change is uncomfortable at times, we do not necessarily need to fear it. I hope that you have also recognised that change is not linear, but a process with highs and lows.

Change can be empowering, allowing us to shed what we no longer need and align ourselves with the essence of who we are. Change can also present opportunities to view ourselves, others and situations with compassion and acceptance, focusing on what is in our control and letting go of what we cannot change.

This book is not intended to provide a 'quick fix'. The aim is to help you to get to know yourself better so that you can create healthier patterns in how you feel, how you think and what you do. In this way, you create a new baseline for your life and can choose to feel and think differently and take more positive inspired actions.

I encourage you to revisit the activities in this book as a way of checking in with yourself and staying focused on that vision of the best possible you. The activities will help you to develop better coping strategies and life skills as you recognise that you are worth investing in.

As we reach the end of the book, I encourage you to reflect on the following:

★ What is my vision for my life...

- In one month?
- In three months?
- In six months?
- In a year?

★ What action steps do I commit to taking to get me closer to my vision?

★ Why do I want to take these actions and what will they give me...

- Mentally?
- Emotionally?
- Physically?
- Spiritually?

★ How will I continue to commit to taking care of and investing in myself, even if I do not feel like it?

I wish you the best as you continue this journey of regularly reconnecting with the real you. I hope you know that you are valued, worthy, unique and powerful.

Additional Resources

Here I have included some helpful resources in the form of grounding, mindfulness and relaxation techniques, affirmation cards and UK-based services and charities that may be of use to you.

Grounding and relaxation techniques

Not all grounding techniques will work for everyone all the time, so finding the right ones may take some trial and error. I recommend trying all the techniques mentioned at least once so that you can get a feel for which you prefer and to have variety in your toolkit to use at different times.

Start by practising one to two grounding techniques a day, just for a short period of time, such as 30 seconds in the morning and 30 seconds in the evening, or tag them onto your everyday activities – when you're brushing your teeth, having a cup of coffee, as part of your bedtime routine. See this as a process of developing new life skills.

Deep breathing

The basis of any relaxation or grounding techniques is deep breathing. This means taking slower, deeper breaths and paying more attention to the way that you breathe. When we are stressed or anxious, our breathing becomes faster and more irregular, we may even hold our breath. This is a simple thing to alter.

To practise deep breathing, start by sitting or standing comfortably and keep your back relatively straight. I always encourage people to take their awareness to their feet on the floor so that they feel grounded. Try to have your shoulders pushed back slightly (but not to the point that you are uncomfortable) to open up your chest area. Notice and pay attention to your breath. Now breathe in through your nose and out through your mouth and continue until you are in a slow and steady rhythm. If you like, you can count in your head to help keep a steady pace. For example, breathing in for one...two... and breathing out for one...two... or saying to yourself in your mind 'I am breathing in for one, I am breathing out for one', 'I am breathing in for two, I am breathing out for two', and so on until you get to ten breaths. You could also imagine breathing in a colour of your choice and imagine it flowing through your body as you breathe in and out. Choose a colour that makes you feel calm and relaxed, or a colour that you like.

Tip: Try not to over-breathe. Instead, focus on *how* you are breathing, how it feels to breathe, noticing your breath. Start by counting to a smaller number while you get used to the technique; you can then build up over time. For example, you could start by breathing in for two and out for two, then in for three and out for three, then in for four and out for four and so on.

Square breathing

This is a variation of the deep breathing technique above. To help you, you can draw a square, look at a square object, trace a square on your leg as you go through the technique or imagine a square in your mind. In this technique, you breathe in (through your nose), hold the breath (so that your stomach expands), breathe out (through your mouth) and hold (your stomach may feel empty). It can take a few goes to get into a rhythm but you will soon find a flow. Remembering the instructions helps you to stay focused and present in the moment. If you like, you can also attach a count to help slow your breathing down, for example, 'Breathe in for one...two... hold for one...two... breathe out for one...two... and hold for one...two...' You should continue to go through the square breathing for at least a few rounds or until you feel calmer and more relaxed.

Smell and/or taste

Smell is a powerful way to bring the body back into the here and now. It can get us out of an anxious mindset and into the present moment, which can help us to be more focused, present and to switch our thinking brains on. Choose a smell that makes you feel calm and relaxed. This could be a favourite perfume or cologne, essential oil, candles, air fresheners, incense – anything. Use this scent to ground you when you are feeling adrift, anxious or overwhelmed by slowly breathing it in.

Similarly, you can use the power of taste to help 'shock' your body. To do this, taste something that's at the extreme end of a taste sensation, for example something extremely sour or sweet. Experiencing the taste sensation brings your awareness back to your body in the now.

Safe space visualisation

This is a visualisation technique to help you to feel calmer, more relaxed and grounded. The first time you go through this visualisation, I recommend you do so in a quiet space where you won't be disturbed for a few minutes, so that you can identify your 'safe space'. This should ideally be somewhere outside of your home. I have created an audio download of this visualisation that is available to access via my website.

You can either read the following script out loud or record yourself saying it so that it becomes your personalised guided meditation:

Sit in a space for a few minutes where you won't be disturbed.

If it feels comfortable to do so, close your eyes. Otherwise, lower your gaze.

Take a deep breath in and out.

If you notice any areas of tension in your body, breathe into them and notice as they feel more relaxed.

Now imagine a space where you feel calm, relaxed and safe.

This can be a place that you have been to before, a place that you have always wanted to visit, a place you have seen an image of or a place that you can imagine in your mind.

Standing in this safe space, look down at your feet and notice the surface that you are standing on. Do you have shoes on, or are you barefoot?

Look ahead of you and around you. Notice all of the colours, objects and shapes that you can see, nearby and in the distance. Take a moment to drink it all in.

You may get a sense of whether you are on your own or if there are other people nearby or in the distance.

Pay attention to what you can hear – are there noises near to you, farther away from you, or is there silence?

Notice what you can touch or feel. What is the temperature like? Can you feel any sensations on your skin, like the clothes you are wearing or the air moving around you?

Can you smell anything? Taste anything?

Really immerse yourself in this safe space and observe the feeling of calm and relaxation flowing through your body.

This is your safe space. Only you have access to this space. If you want to, you can give your space a name.

Take a moment here.

Now take a breath in and out. Feel your feet on the ground in the room that you are currently in and slowly and gently open your eyes, in your own time.

Once you have identified your safe space, you can repeat this exercise again, going through the same process and imagining yourself in your safe space using all of your senses.

Mindfulness techniques

Mindfulness techniques are a way of noticing what is happening in your mind, body and the world around you. Below are some easy-to-use techniques:

Colour/object spotting

First, pick a colour. For the next few minutes, look around your environment and notice anything that is that colour or has that colour in it. The aim is to help you to be more present in your surroundings. This technique can be repeated with objects, as 'object spotting', noticing the big and small objects that you can see around you.

Fresh perspective

Pick up an object that you use every day (eg, pen, pencil, book etc). For the next two minutes, focus on this object, giving it your full attention. What do you notice about it? Can you notice something new about this object today?

Five senses

This is a quick mindfulness exercise that you can do to bring your awareness back to this moment and your environment.

★   Focus on five things that you can see

★   Focus on four things that you can hear

★   Focus on three things that you can touch

★   Focus on two things that you can smell

★   Focus on one thing that you can taste

Body scan

Below is a script for a body scan exercise. You can also listen to an audio version of this script via my website.

1. Sit in a comfortable position and close your eyes if this feels comfortable, or lower your gaze.

2. Take three breaths in and out. Check in with your body, noticing any sensations and feeling contact with the floor.

3. Now start scanning your body and noticing the different parts. You are not going to judge what you are thinking or feeling, just be still and notice it.

    -   To start with, pay attention to your face and head. Can you feel anything here (eg, tingling, numbness, tightness, warmth, coldness)? Do you notice anything in your mind? Is your face relaxed or scrunched up? How do the various features on your face feel – your eyes, nose, mouth? Can you hear or smell anything?

- Now move your attention to the neck and shoulders. How do they feel?

- Now move into your upper arms. Do they feel heavy or relaxed? Are your hands hot or cold?

4. Take one more deep breath and pay attention to your whole body. What does it feel like? How do you feel when you breathe in and out?

5. Take a final deep breath in and out. When you are ready, open your eyes and come back into the room.

Progressive muscle relaxation

Progressive muscle relaxation is where you tense and relax certain muscle groups while coordinating your breathing in and out. There are many ways this can be done; I have outlined one simple way below:

★ Take a deep breath in and out.

★ Imagine you have a stress ball in the palm of your hand.

★ Squeeze the stress ball as hard as you can and breathe in while you do this.

★ Now breathe out and open your hands, imagining the stress ball returning to its original shape.

★ Repeat this five more times.

Creating your symbol of empowerment

Think of an inner strength that you have or would like to have more of – for example, confidence, compassion, kindness or resilience.

Take an A4 piece of paper and a pen. With your non-dominant hand (the hand that you do not write with), and without thinking too much, draw a symbol that represents this strength. Don't worry about the quality of the drawing – this is about the process.

Once you have drawn your power symbol, put your piece of paper on the floor. Then stand up and notice how you are currently feeling in your body – what is your posture like? What sensations are you experiencing in your body? How does your mind feel? What is your body temperature like? Is your body tense or relaxed?

Now step onto your power symbol and visualise it connecting with your body and amplifying the strength that it represents. Notice how different your body feels when you step into this strength. Solidify this feeling by saying in your head or aloud, 'I am [the strength you identified].'

Remember, you can use this technique again by imagining that you are stepping back onto your power symbol and reconnecting with how your body feels when you are in your power.

Your toolkit

As you go on your journey, add any other positive coping strategies you develop or discover into your toolkit, so that you have them to hand.

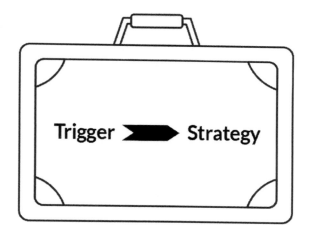

Affirmation cards

Many people find affirmations or strength-based statements a helpful way to stay positive and focused. Why not create some cards with your chosen affirmations written or printed on them. You could randomly pick an affirmation for each day in order to stay focused on your goals. My tip is to keep the cards somewhere you can see (or take a picture of them), so that you remember to recite them throughout the day. Say them aloud or in your mind as many times as you need to.

Try and make these affirmations values-based and relevant to who you are as a person. For example, they
could be based on your character (eg, 'I have inner
strength', 'I am a compassionate person') or linked
to your personal goals (eg, 'I am successful', 'I have
the inner and outer resources I need', 'I love myself
unconditionally'). Make your affirmations as specific
as possible, use the present tense and try to avoid
negative statements. For example, rather than 'I am
not fearful', a more positive statement would be 'I am
fearless'.

My affirmations/positive statements

You can also create your own affirmations. A blank
template for creating your own can be downloaded
via my website.

List of useful organisations in the UK

There may be times when it is useful to speak to someone or find more information. Below I have listed some organisations in the UK that may be of use to you. Please note, you can and should speak to your GP or medical professional in charge of your care for advice on physical and mental health concerns; they will be able to make referrals to appropriate services.

Urgent help/crisis support

If you, or someone you know, is in immediate danger, then you should call emergency services or go to the nearest A&E.

The following services also offer crisis helplines:

★ **Samaritans** – confidential support for people experiencing feelings of distress or despair. Phone: 116 123 (free 24-hour helpline). Website: www.samaritans.org.uk.

★ **Childline** – Childline is a UK counselling service for children and young people up to their nineteenth birthday, provided by the NSPCC. Phone: 0800 1111 (free 24-hour helpline). Website: www.childline.org.uk.

The following services offer support for issues related to domestic abuse:

★ **Refuge National Domestic Abuse Helpline**.
Phone: 0808 200 0247.
Website: www.nationaldahelpline.org.uk.

★ **Respect Men's Advice Line** – for male domestic
abuse survivors. Phone: 0808 801 0327. Website:
https://mensadviceline.org.uk.

★ **The Mix** – free support and information for under-25s.
Phone: 0808 808 4994. Website: www.themix.org.uk.

★ **Galop National LGBTQI+ Domestic Abuse
Helpline**. Phone: 0800 999 5428. Website:
https://galop.org.uk/get-help/helpline

★ **Women's Aid**. Website: www.womensaid.org.uk.

Additional resources

★ **Anxiety UK** – charity providing support for
people diagnosed with an anxiety condition.
Phone: 03444 775 774 (Monday to Friday, 9.30am
to 5.30pm). Website: www.anxietyuk.org.uk.

★ **CALM** – CALM is the Campaign Against Living
Miserably. Phone: 0800 585 858 (daily, 5pm to
midnight). Website: www.thecalmzone.net.

★ **Mental Health Foundation** – provides information and support for anyone with mental health problems or learning disabilities. Website: www.mentalhealth.org.uk.

★ **Mind** – promotes the views and needs of people with mental health problems. Phone: 0300 123 3393 (Monday to Friday, 9am to 6pm). Website: www.mind.org.uk.

★ **PAPYRUS** – young suicide prevention society. Phone: HOPElineUK 0800 068 4141 (Monday to Friday, 10am to 5pm and 7pm to 10pm, and 2pm to 5pm on weekends). Website: www.papyrus-uk.org.

★ **Rethink Mental Illness** – support and advice for people living with mental illness. Phone: 0300 5000 927 (Monday to Friday, 9.30am to 4pm). Website: www.rethink.org.

★ **SANE** – emotional support, information and guidance for people affected by mental illness, their families and carers. SANEline: 0300 304 7000 (daily, 4.30pm to 10.30pm). Textcare: comfort and care via text message, sent when the person needs it most: www.sane.org.uk/textcare. Peer support forum: www.sane.org.uk/supportforum. Website: www.sane.org.uk/support.

★ **YoungMinds** – information on child and adolescent mental health. Services for parents and professionals.
Phone: parents' helpline 0808 802 5544 (Monday to Friday, 9.30am to 4pm).
Website: www.youngminds.org.uk.

Please note that these service details were correct at the time of publishing, but this may change over time. For an up-to-date list of mental health services in the UK, visit www.nhs.uk.

Private therapy

If you are searching for a private psychologist or therapist within the UK, the following websites may be helpful (please note that this is not an exhaustive list):

★ The Health & Care Professions Council – www.hcpc-uk.org

★ The British Psychological Society – www.bps.org.uk

★ British Association for Counselling and Psychotherapy – www.bacp.co.uk

★ Association for Family Therapy and Systemic Practice – www.aft.org.uk

★ British Association for Behavioural and Cognitive Psychotherapies – www.babcp.com

If you are registered with a private insurance company, they may also be able to provide you with support, depending on your level of cover.

References And Bibliography

Ainsworth, M, Bell, SM (1970). Attachment, exploration, and separation: Illustrated by the behavior of one-year-olds in a strange situation. *Child Development*, 41(1), 49–67.

Ainsworth, M, and Blehar, M, Waters, E, et al. (1978). *Patterns of Attachment: A psychological study of the strange situation.* Lawrence Erlbaum Associates.

Annett, M (1985). *Left, Right, Hand and Brain: The right shift theory* (pp. 205). Lawrence Erlbaum Associates.

Barlow, DH (2002). *Anxiety and Its Disorders.* Guilford Press.

Beck, AT (1964). Thinking and depression: II. Theory and therapy. *Archives of General Psychiatry*, 10(6), 561–571.

Beck, AT (1976). *Cognitive Therapy and the Emotional Disorders.* International Universities Press.

Beck, AT (2005). The current state of cognitive therapy: A 40-year retrospective. *Archives of General Psychiatry*, 62(9), 953–959.

Beck, AT (2008). The evolution of the cognitive model of depression and its neurobiological correlates. *American Journal of Psychiatry*, 165(8), 969–977.

Beck, AT, Rush, J, Shaw, B, et al. (1979). *Cognitive Therapy of Depression.* Guilford Press.

Beck, JS (2005). *Cognitive Therapy for Challenging Problems: What to do when the basics don't work.* Guilford Press.

Bloch, D (2015). *Positive Self-Talk for Children: Teaching self-esteem through affirmations.* Bookbaby.

Bowlby, J (1969). *Attachment and Loss: Volume I. Attachment.* Hogarth Press.

Bowlby, J (1982). Attachment and loss: Retrospect and prospect. *American Journal of Orthopsychiatry*, 52(4), 664–678.

Capacchione, L (2019). *The Power of Your Other Hand: Unlock creativity and inner wisdom through the right side of your brain.* Conari Press.

Cascio, CN, O'Donnell, MB, Tinney, et al. (2015). Self-affirmation activates brain systems associated with self-related processing and reward and is reinforced by future orientation. *Social Cognitive and Affective Neuroscience*, 11(4), 621–629.

Casey, BJ, Giedd, JN, and Thomas, KM (2000). Structural and functional brain development and its relation to cognitive development. *Biological Psychiatry*, 54(1–3), 241–257.

Chen, Q, Yang, H, Rooks, B, et al. (2020). Autonomic flexibility reflects learning and associated neuroplasticity in old age. *Human Brain Mapping*, 41(13), 3608–3619.

Cohen, GL, and Sherman, DK (2014). The psychology of change: Self-affirmation and social psychological intervention. *Annual Review of Psychology*, 65, 333–371.

Cooke, R, Trebaczyk, H, Harris, P, et al. (2014). Self-affirmation promotes physical activity. *Journal of Sport and Exercise Psychology*, 36(2), 217–223.

Critcher, CR, and Dunning, D (2015). Self-affirmations provide a broader perspective on self-threat. *Personality and Social Psychology Bulletin*, 41(1), 3–18.

Draper, P, and Belsky, J (1990). Personality development in the evolutionary perspective. *Journal of Personality*, 58(1), 141–161.

Ellis, A (2003). Cognitive restructuring of the disputing of irrational beliefs. In WT O'Donohue and JE Fisher (Eds.), *Cognitive Behavior Therapy: Applying empirically supported techniques in your practice*, 2nd edition (pp. 79–83). Wiley.

Feltham, C, and Dryden, W (1993). *Dictionary of Counselling*. Whurr Publishers.

Gilbert, P, Clarke, M, Kempel, S, et al. (2004). Criticizing and reassuring oneself: An exploration of forms, style and reasons in female students. *British Journal of Clinical Psychology*, 43 (Pt 1), 31–50.

Gilbert, P, Durrant, R, and McEwan, K (2006). Investigating relationships between perfectionism, forms and functions of self-criticism, and sensitivity to put-down. *Personality and Individual Differences*, 41(7), 1299–1308.

Greenberger, D, and Padesky, C (1995). *Mind Over Mood: Changing how you feel by changing the way you think.* Guilford Press.

Hölzel BK, Carmody J, Vangel M, et al. (2011). Mindfulness practice leads to increases in regional brain gray matter density. *Psychiatry Research*, 191(1), 36–43.

Hölzel BK, Carmody J, Evans KC, et al. (2010). Stress reduction correlates with structural changes in the amygdala. *Social Cognitive and Affective Neuroscience*, 5(1), 11–17.

Kabat-Zinn, J (1982). An outpatient program in behavioral medicine for chronic pain patients based on the practice of mindfulness meditation: Theoretical considerations and preliminary results. *General Hospital Psychiatry*, 4(1), 33–47.

Kaczmarek, B (2020). Current views on neuroplasticity: What is new and what is old? *Acta Neuropsychologica*, 18(1), 1–14.

Linehan, M, (1993). *Cognitive Behavioural Therapy of Borderline Personality Disorder.* Guilford Press.

Linehan, M (2014). *DBT Training Manual.* Guilford Press.

Linehan, M, and Kehrer, CA (1993). Borderline personality disorder. In DH Barlow (Ed.), *Clinical Handbook of Psychological Disorders: A step-by-step treatment manual* (pp. 396–441). Guilford Press.

Lyons-Ruth, K (1996). Attachment relationships among children with aggressive behavior problems: The role of disorganized early attachment patterns. *Journal of Consultant Clinical Psychology*, 64(1), 64–73.

Main, M, and Solomon, J (1986). Discovery of an insecure-disorganized/disoriented attachment pattern. In TB Brazelton and MW Yogman (Eds.), *Affective Development in Infancy* (pp. 95–124). Ablex Publishing.

NICE (2011). CG123: Common Mental Health Disorders: Identification and Pathways to Care.

Philip, BA, and Frey, SH (2016). Increased functional connectivity between cortical hand areas and praxis network associated with training-related improvements in non-dominant hand precision drawing. *Neuropsychologica*, 87, 157–168.

Poerio, GL, Sormaz, M, Wang, HT, et al. (2017). The role of the default mode network in component processes underlying the wandering mind. *Social Cognitive and Affective Neuroscience*, 12(7), 1047–1062.

Saigh, PA, and Bremner, JD (1999). *Posttraumatic Stress Disorder: A comprehensive text.* Allyn & Bacon.

Seligman, L (2006). *Theories of Counselling and Psychotherapy: Systems, strategies, and skills.* Pearson Prentice Hall.

Shalev, AY, Peri, T, Caneti, L, et al. (1996). Predictors of PTSD in injured trauma survivors: A prospective study. *American Journal of Psychiatry*, 153(2), 219–225.

Tahmasian, M, Samea, F, Khazaie, H, et al. (2020). The interrelation of sleep and mental and physical health is anchored in grey-matter neuroanatomy and under genetic control. *Communications Biology*, 3(1), 171.

Van Der Kolk, BA (2000). The diagnosis and treatment of Complex PTSD. In R Yehuda (Ed.), *Current Treatment of PTSD.* American Psychiatric Press.

Van Der Kolk, BA, Pelcovitz, D, Roth, S, et al. (1996). Dissociation, somatization, and affect dysregulation: The complexity of adaptation to trauma. *American Journal of Psychiatry*, 153(7,suppl), 83–93.

Waters, E, Weinfield, NS, and Hamilton, CE (2000). The stability of attachment security from infancy to adolescence and early adulthood: General discussion. *Child Development*, 71(3), 703–706.

Waters, E, Merrick, S, Treboux, D, et al. (2000). Attachment security in infancy and early adulthood: A twenty-year longitudinal study. *Child Development*, 71(3), 684–689.

The Author

Dr Rina Bajaj is a British-Asian Chartered Counselling Psychologist with over seventeen years' clinical experience within the field of mental health and wellbeing. She runs two award-winning practices servicing diverse communities in London and has previously worked in the NHS, led on government projects within schools and higher education, worked in grass roots charities and held various consultancy roles within the corporate sector.

Rina has worked with many interesting clients over the years including entrepreneurs, millionaires and billionaires, celebrities, TV personalities, professional athletes, musicians and artists. Rina is naturally empathetic and always wanted to be in a profession that could support people to make positive changes. She is a great believer in experiencing new things and believes that if she asks her clients to step out of their comfort zone, then she must be prepared to do the same.

She provides individual and relationship therapy, business consultation, coaching and executive coaching. She is an expert in childhood and adult trauma, children and young people's mental health, anxiety, low mood, depression, confidence, self-esteem, identity and relationships. She has worked with many global companies providing consultation, workshops and training on areas including staff wellbeing, mental health awareness, diversity, mindfulness, mindset, motivation, habit-building and stress management.

Rina is a regular contributor to national media and is a confident presenter, having spoken at national and international emotional wellbeing conferences aimed at a range of professionals. Her recent media contributions can be viewed here: https://linktr.ee/drrinabajaj

🌐 www.rinabajaj.com

📷 @Dr.Rina.Bajaj

🐦 @DrRinaBajaj